Tears in a Bottle

Printed September 2007
The Graphix Network
4104-C Colben Blvd.
Evans, Georgia
(706) 210-1000

Cover photography:

Kyle Shell of Lawrence 𝒦 photography

ISBN # 978-0-9795623-1-0

Remember Yahushua's Tears!

Psalms 56

Thou take account of my mournings: put my tears into thy bottle: Are they not in thy book? When I cry unto thee, then shall mine enemies turn back: this I know; for Elohim is for Me. In Elohim will I praise His word: In ⴶYⴶz will I praise His word. In Elohim have I put my trust: I will not be afraid what man can do unto me. Thy vows are upon Me, O Elohim: I will render praises unto thee. For You have delivered my soul from death: wilt not thou deliver my feet from falling, that I may walk before Elohim in the light of the living?

The Furnace of Affliction

When you are put in the Furnace of Affliction, meditate on Romans 8!

And we know that **all things** work together for good to them that love ⲀⲨⲀⱫ, to them who are the called according to His purpose. For whom He did foreknow, He also did predestinate to be conformed to the image of His Son, that He might be the firstborn among many brothers. Moreover whom He did predestinate, them He also called: and whom He called, them He also justified: and whom He justified, them He also glorified. What shall we then say to these things? If ⲀⲨⲀⱫ be for us, who can be against us? He that spared not his own Son, but delivered Him up for us all, how shall He not with Him also freely give us all things? Who shall lay any thing to the charge of Yahuah's elect? It is ⲀⲨⲀⱫ that justifieth. Who is he that condemneth? It is the Messiah that died, yes rather, that is raised again, who is even at the right hand of ⲀⲨⲀⱫ, who also maketh intercession for us. Who shall separate us from the love of the Messiah? Shall tribulation, or distress, or persecution, or famine, or nakedness, or peril, or sword? As it is written, for thy sake we are killed all the day long; we are accounted as sheep for the slaughter. No, in all these things we are **more than conquerors** through Him that loved us.

Table of Contents

A Thankful Heart

Dear **OWYƎZ** my Beloved, if I said thank you a thousand times over, it could not express the love and thankfulness in my heart for You! In the abundance of your mercy and compassion, You have set my feet on the narrow Way and opened my eyes to see the real **OWYƎZ**! Thank You for giving me the privilege of retelling your story! May You open the hearts and minds of your sheep so that they can see Your tears! When they see, they will weep! May *Tears in a Bottle* help Israel to overcome the utter darkness in this present world, just as You did!

Thank You OWYƎZ!

Todah OWYƎZ! Todah OWYƎZ! Todah OWYƎZ!

Preface

Tears in a Bottle restores truth forgotten long ago about Yahushua's sojourn on earth as Israel's Passover Lamb! Yahushua is the anointed one of ᴀYᴀZ, who came to save mankind from the penalty of their sins! Yahushua's set apart name is written in Paleo (ancient) Hebrew as OWYᴀZ! OWYᴀZ is transliterated into English as Yahushua **(Ya-hoo-shoo-ah)**. OWYᴀZ is the heavenly Father's provision for the salvation of every soul, who has ever lived! When transliterated into English, the heavenly Father's name is Yahuah **(Ya-hoo-wah)**! In Paleo Hebrew Yahuah is written as ᴀYᴀZ! All the sons of Adam, who have ever lived and chosen to love and honor ᴀYᴀZ, are called Israel! Those called Israel will strive with OWYᴀZ in this world, will overcome with OWYᴀZ in this world, and will rule with OWYᴀZ in the world to come! ᴀYᴀZ and OWYᴀZ are the two most important names **ever** named! The Way of salvation can only be obtained through those two names and **none other**! OWYᴀZ was sent by ᴀYᴀZ as the Passover Lamb appointed for Israel's salvation! OWYᴀZ **was perfectly willing** to completely humble Himself in a body of mortal flesh to suffer for the sins of others! Then at the appointed time, OWYᴀZ chose to end His own life by hanging on a cursed tree, **not for His own sins**, **but for the sins of others**! OWYᴀZ was willing to suffer horrific afflictions, insults, rejections, betrayals, and finally a cursed death on a tree, all because **He had a dream**! Yahushua's dream was that by His suffering, He would bring many brothers and sisters into the family of Elohim! But during the time of Constantine, a big **switch-r-rue** occurred! Constantine used his great power as the Roman Emperor to change the real physical image of the OWYᴀZ into the Greek image of perfect beauty! Constantine also changed Yahuah's set apart times, mixed unclean pagan traditions with clean Scriptural themes, and created separation between Jewish and gentile believers! For nearly 1,700 years religious and secular powers in this world have added to the confusion surrounding OWYᴀZ! The set apart names of OWYᴀZ and ᴀYᴀZ are still largely unknown or suppressed in many places! Those names are blasphemed and disrespected all over this world each and every day! For nearly 2,000 years the words of OWYᴀZ have been twisted, perverted, and ignored by multitudes of false shepherds and their blinded sheep!

Tears in a Bottle

Millions of sheep have been led astray by wolf shepherds, who have fleeced their own sheep for their own personal gain! Countless sheep have gone to their graves believing that all is well, when in reality they were **spiritually naked**! However, there has always been a remnant of overcomers, who ᴀYᴀℤ calls Israel! My purpose for writing *Tears in a Bottle* is to feed the overcomers of Israel by restoring the truth about Yahushua's **suffering** and Yahushua's **overcoming**! All the faithful of heart will be pricked by Yahuah's set apart Spirit (His Ruach HaQodesh), when they read *Tears in a Bottle*! **Nothing could be closer to the heart of ᴀYᴀℤ, than the tears of OWYᴀℤ!** Remember the question posed by YeshaYahu (Isaiah) in Isaiah 53! "Who has believed our report?" Today as you read *Tears in a Bottle,* please consider these questions. Does anybody care about Yahushua's feelings? Does anybody today even care about the unspeakable pain, rejection, and humiliation that OWYᴀℤ actually suffered? Does anybody care about Yahushua's hopes and dreams for Israel's future? I know that there is a remnant of Israel, who does care very deeply! **They will weep as I have wept, when they know the mystery of OWYᴀℤ!** On the Day of ᴀYᴀℤ, OWYᴀℤ will gather His people called Israel back to the wilderness ruins of Yahrushalayim in the **real** Promised Land! There OWYᴀℤ will reveal Himself and cut a **New Covenant** with the faithful! When they see Him, **then Israel will weep and weep and weep!**

Zekaryah 13
And they shall look on Me, whom they pierced, and they shall mourn for Him as one mourns for his only son. And they shall be in bitterness over Him as bitterness over the first-born.

Tears in a Bottle attempts to restore the real **magnitude** of Yahushua's suffering! However, mere words fail to hit the mark because they **cannot** adequately describe Yahushua's agony! It's vital that Israel understand Yahushua's suffering, but it's equally important that Israel understand how OWYᴀℤ **overcame**! To overcome the world today, Israel must apply Yahushua's pattern for overcoming to their own lives! **Finish well!** Follow Yahushua's example for overcoming in this world by trusting in ᴀYᴀℤ **alone for your deliverance! When ᴀYᴀℤ tests the reins of your heart by placing you in His Furnace of Affliction, first remember Yahushua's tears and then remember Yahushua's victory!**

May ᴀYᴀℤ bless you and let you see His face, OWYᴀℤ!

Chapter 1
The Child of the Promise

[15]"And I put enmity between you and the woman, and between your seed and her Seed. He shall crush your head, and you shall crush His heel." Genesis 3

On the day Adam and Hawwah (Eve) first sinned, ᴣΥᴣ꒱ promised Adam that He would raise a Deliverer from Adam's seed, who would crush the head of the serpent. That promise was a great comfort to Adam, who was extremely remorseful because of his sin and his subsequent expulsion from the Garden on the heavenly Mount Zion. Since that time, all of Yahuah's sheep, who ᴣΥᴣ꒱ calls Israel, have looked forward to the coming of their Deliverer! When our Deliverer, EliYahu, the mighty one of ᴣΥᴣ꒱ came, the heavenly messenger, Gabriel instructed Joseph to name Yahuah's Deliverer, OWYᴣ꒱! Sadly, when OWYᴣ꒱ came first as Israel's Passover Lamb, most of the sheep of Israel were completely blinded to the truth about His identity! The Prophets had written that an anointed one was to come from the line of King David and He was to be born in Beth Lehem of Yahudah. In spite of all this, when OWYᴣ꒱ did come, multitudes of Israel's sheep were completely blinded to the real truth of His identity. **They did not recognize Him** as the anointed one of ᴣΥᴣ꒱! **Why didn't they get it?** That's the billion dollar question! The people were expecting the anointed one, but they had false expectations about His coming. They were expecting a warrior king like David, who would break the yoke of the Rome and restore the former glory back to Israel! But the real OWYᴣ꒱ became a stumbling block to the sheep of Israel! Why didn't they recognize Him? Why, why, why, what really happened? Let's go back and look to the prophets of ᴣΥᴣ꒱ for clues about the coming of OWYᴣ꒱.

Deuteronomy 18 (Moses)
*I will raise them up a Prophet (OWYᴣ꒱) from among their brethren, like unto thee, and will put my words in his mouth; and He shall speak unto them all that I shall command him. And it shall come to pass, that whosoever will not hearken unto my words which He shall speak in **my name (ᴣΥᴣ꒱)**, I will require it of him.*

Jeremiah 23
Behold, the days come, saith ⟨AYƎZ⟩, that I will raise unto __David__ a __righteous__ Branch (OWYƎZ), and a King shall reign and prosper, and shall execute judgment and justice in the earth (on the Day of ⟨AYƎZ⟩)

Micah 5
"But you, __Beyth Lehem__ Ephrathah, you who are little among the clans of Yehudah, out of you shall come forth to Me the One (OWYƎZ) to become Ruler in Yisra'el. And His comings forth are of old, from everlasting." [3]Therefore He shall give them up, until the time that she who is in labor has given birth (Revelation 12), and the remnant of His brothers return to the children of Yisra'el. [4]And He shall stand and shepherd in the strength of ⟨AYƎZ⟩, in the excellency of the Name of ⟨AYƎZ⟩ His Elohim. And they shall dwell for at that time He shall be great to the ends of the earth.

Isaiah 11
And there shall come forth a __rod__ (OWYƎZ) out of the stem of Jesse (King David's line), and a Branch shall grow out of his roots: and the __spirit__ of ⟨AYƎZ⟩ shall rest upon Him, the spirit of wisdom and understanding, the spirit of counsel and might, the spirit of knowledge and of the fear of ⟨AYƎZ⟩; and shall make Him of quick understanding in the fear of ⟨AYƎZ⟩: and He shall __not judge after the sight of his eyes, neither reprove after the hearing of his ears__: But with righteousness shall He judge the poor, and reprove with equity for the meek of the earth: and He shall smite the earth with the rod of His mouth, and with the breath of His lips shall He slay the wicked. And righteousness shall be the girdle of His loins, and faithfulness the girdle of His reins.

Isaiah 9
Nevertheless the dimness shall not be such as was in her vexation, when at the first He lightly afflicted the land of Zebulun and the land of Naphtali, and afterward did more grievously afflict her by the way of the sea, beyond Jordan, in Galilee of the nations. The people that walked in darkness have seen a great light (OWYƎZ): they that dwell in the land of the shadow of death, upon them hath the light (OWYƎZ) shined. Thou hast multiplied the nation, and not increased the joy: they joy before thee according to the joy in harvest, and as men rejoice when they divide the spoil.

Isaiah 9, cont.
For thou hast broken the yoke of his burden, and the staff of his shoulder, the rod of his oppressor, as in the day of Midian. For every battle of the warrior is with confused noise, and garments rolled in blood; but this shall be with burning and fuel of fire. **For unto us a child (OWYƎⱿ) is born, unto us a Son is given: and the government shall be upon his shoulder: and His name shall be called Wonderful, Counselor, the mighty El, the everlasting Father, the Prince of Peace.** *Of the increase of his government and peace there shall be no end, upon the throne of David, and upon his kingdom, to order it, and to establish it with judgment and with justice from henceforth even for ever.*

Malachi 4
Behold, I will send you EliYah **(the mighty one of Yah; OWYƎⱿ)** *the prophet before the coming of the great and dreadful Day of ⱯYƎⱿ: and He (OWYƎⱿ) shall turn the heart of the fathers to the children, and the heart of the children to their fathers, lest I come and smite the earth with a curse.*

Matthew 2
And thou **Bethlehem**, *in the land of Yahudah, art not the least among the princes of Yahudah: for out of thee shall come a* **governor (OWYƎⱿ), that shall rule my people Israel.**

The Book of Adam and Eve is an ancient spiritual writing, but it was not canonized by man. However, I believe that *The Book of Adam and Eve* is certainly worth reading and meditating on. Read it! You'll enjoy it! Evaluate it for yourself. It contains a treasure trove of information about events, before the Flood.

Book of Adam and Eve
Chapter 3 *Concerning the promise of the great five and a half days. 1 ⱯYƎⱿ said to Adam, "I have ordained on this earth days and years, and you and your descendants shall live and walk in them, until the days and years are fulfilled; when I shall send the Word (OWYƎⱿ) that created you, and against which you have transgressed, the Word (OWYƎⱿ) that made you come out of the garden, and that raised you when you were fallen. Yes, the Word (OWYƎⱿ) that will again save you when the five and a half days are fulfilled." But when Adam heard these words from ⱯYƎⱿ, and of the great five and a half days, he did not understand the meaning of them.*

Book of Adam and Eve

Chapter 3, cont.
For Adam was thinking there would be only five and a half days for him until the end of the world. And Adam cried, and prayed to ᴀYᴀZ to explain it to him. Then ᴀYᴀZ in His mercy for Adam, who was made after His own image and likeness, explained to him, that these were 5,000 and 500 years; **and how one would then come and save him and his descendants.**

Chapter 21
And said to Adam, "O Adam, all this misery which you have brought on yourself, will have no affect against my rule, neither will it alter the **covenant of the 5,500 years***.*

Chapter 22
Then the merciful ᴀYᴀZ, good and lover of men, looked at Adam and Eve, and at their blood, which they had held up as an offering to Him; without an order from Him for so doing. But He wondered at them; and accepted their offerings. And ᴀYᴀZ sent from His presence a bright fire, that consumed their offering. He smelled the sweet savor of their offering, and showed them mercy. Then came (OWYᴀZ) the Word of ᴀYᴀZ to Adam, and said to him, "O Adam, as you have shed your blood, so will I shed my own blood, when I become flesh of your descendants; and as you died, O Adam, so also will I die. And as you built an altar, so also will I make for you an altar of the earth; and as you offered your blood on it, so also will I offer My blood on an altar on the earth. And as you sued for forgiveness through that blood, so also will I make my blood forgiveness of sins, and erase transgressions in it. And now, behold, I have accepted your offering, O Adam, but the 'days' of the covenant in which I have bound you are not fulfilled. **When they are fulfilled, then will I bring you back into the Garden.**

His Name shall be called OWYᴀZ!

The anointed one of Yahuah was named OWYᴀZ in the honor of His Father's name! OWYᴀZ came in His Father's name, ᴀYᴀZ! Reading from right to left, anyone can see that the first three Hebrew letters (Yod-hey-waw) are the same in both the Father's name and the Son's name (YᴀZ; transliterated into English as Yahu or Yah). The letter "J" as in Jesus was **not** established until **1,600** years latter.

Obviously the Messiah's real name was **not** Jesus! The word Jesus comes from a Greek and Latin hybrid, Ieous, which still appears in early English translations before the year 1600. Please, do your own research on the set apart (Qodesh) names of 𐤉𐤄𐤅𐤄 and 𐤉𐤄𐤅𐤔𐤏! **On judgment Day, you won't be sorry**! A love for the Father's and the Son's Qodesh names is a door that opens to everlasting life!

Acts 2
[21]*'And it shall be that everyone who calls on the Name of 𐤉𐤄𐤅𐤄 shall be saved.*

If you really study, then You will discover that the Messiah's name is in fact 𐤉𐤄𐤅𐤔𐤏! 𐤉𐤄𐤅𐤄 and 𐤉𐤄𐤅𐤔𐤏 are the two most important names ever named in the Heavens, on the Earth, or under the Earth! These two set apart names are the **only** names through which a man, woman, or child can be saved!

Luke 2
[21]*And when eight days were completed for Him to be circumcised, His Name was called 𐤉𐤄𐤅𐤔𐤏, the name given by the messenger before He was conceived in the womb.*

Matthew 1
*Now the birth of 𐤉𐤄𐤅𐤔𐤏 the Messiah was on this wise: When as his mother Mary was espoused to Joseph, before they came together, she was found with child of the Holy Spirit. Then Joseph her husband, being a just man, and not willing to make her a public example, was minded to put her away privily. But while he thought on these things, behold, the messenger of 𐤉𐤄𐤅𐤄 appeared unto him in a dream, saying, Joseph, thou son of David, fear not to take unto thee Mary thy wife: for that which is conceived in her is of the Holy Spirit. And she shall bring forth a son, and **thou shalt call His name** 𐤉𐤄𐤅𐤔𐤏: for He shall save his people from their sins. Now all this was done, that it might be fulfilled which was spoken of 𐤉𐤄𐤅𐤄 by the prophet, saying, behold, a virgin shall be with child, and shall bring forth a son, and they shall call His name Emmanuel, which being interpreted is, Elohim with us.*

Luke 1
[31]*"And see, you shall conceive in your womb, and shall give birth to a Son, and call His name 𐤉𐤄𐤅𐤔𐤏.* [32]*"He shall be great, and shall be called the Son of the Most High.*

Luke 1, cont.
And 𐤀𐤉𐤅𐤀 Elohim shall give Him the throne of His father Dawid.
[33]*"And He shall reign over the house of Ya'aqob forever, and **there shall be no end to His reign.**"*[34]*And Miryam said to the messenger, "How shall this be, since I do not know a man?"* [35]*And the messenger answering, said to her, "The Set-apart Spirit shall come upon you, and the power of the Most High shall overshadow you. And for that reason the Set-apart One born of you shall be called: Son of Elohim.*

From the womb OWY𐤀Z was zealous for His father and was taught by 𐤀Y𐤀Z! From birth Yahushua's appearance was imperfect by the world's superficial standards! OWY𐤀Z did **not** have a handsome countenance! He was **not** a hunk at all, which I can clearly identify with! He had red hair, moles, freckles, and was probably shorter, just like King David. 𐤀Y𐤀Z **does not judge by outward appearances**, but He judges value by the heart! **Had Israel not judged OWY𐤀Z by His outward appearance, they would not have been blinded to the truth about their Deliverer!**

1 Shemu'el (Samuel) 16
[7]*But 𐤀Y𐤀Z said to Shemu'el, "Do **not** look at his appearance or at the height of his stature, because I have refused him (David's brother Eliyab), for not as man sees, **for man looks on the outward appearance, but 𐤀Y𐤀Z looks at the heart.**"*

1 Shemu'el (Samuel) 16
[12]*And he sent and brought him in (David). And he was ruddy, with bright eyes, and good looking. And 𐤀Y𐤀Z said, "Arise, anoint him, for this is the one!"* **(This verse is mistranslated- It should be neither instead of "with":** [12]***And he (David) was ruddy (or red) and neither had he a handsome countenance.***

Dead Sea Scrolls 4Q534
₁*[...] of his hand, two [...] a mark. His hair will be **red** and He will have **moles** on [...] ₁ and small marks in his thighs. [And after t]wo years, He will know one thing from another. **While He is young, He will be like ...[...like] someone who knows nothing, until He ₅knows the three Books [...] Then He will gain wisdom and learn understanding [...] visions will come to him while He is on his knees. ₁ And with His father and ancestors [...] life and old age. He will have wisdom and discretion and He will know the secrets of man. His wisdom will reach out to everyone and He will know the secrets of all living things.***

Dead Sea Scrolls 4Q534, cont.

All of their plans against Him (OWYƏZ) will fail, and His rule over all things will be great. 10[...] His plans will succeed because **He (OWYƏZ) is the one picked by** ƏYƏZ. *His birth and the breath of his spirit [...] and His plans will last forever.*

It is obvious that OWYƏZ was **extremely zealous** for ƏYƏZ **from His very conception!** By the time He was twelve, OWYƏZ had acquired great wisdom and understanding about the Torah directly from ƏYƏZ! ƏYƏZ was Yahushua's teacher! OWYƏZ was so full of Yahuah's wisdom that He was able to completely amaze the wisest Torah scholars in all of Israel! Consider Luke's account of the twelve year old OWYƏZ and His pilgrimage with His family to Yahrushalayim for the Passover celebration! After reading the passage, it should be clear to everyone that OWYƏZ honored the Passover! Shouldn't we also honor the Passover? The Passover is one of seven eternal festivals set apart in Leviticus 23 by ƏYƏZ! They are applicable to all men, forever! OWYƏZ did **not** honor Christmas, Easter, Valentine's Day, or Halloween, because all those festivals are contaminated with pagan practices and origins. **Contrary to popular opinion it does matter to** ƏYƏZ! **Clean is clean and unclean is unclean!** On that day long ago OWYƏZ stayed behind because He was so zealous for ƏYƏZ! Later OWYƏZ was found by His worried parents teaching the Torah scholars instead of the scholars teaching Him! The Torah scholars were astonished at Yahushua's knowledge and authority!

Luke 2
And when they had fulfilled the days, as they returned, the child OWYƏZ *tarried behind in* Yahrushalayim; *and Joseph and his mother knew not of it. But they, supposing Him to have been in the company, went a day's journey; and they sought Him among their kinsfolk and acquaintance. And when they found Him not, they turned back again to* Yahrushalayim, *seeking Him. And it came to pass, that after three days they found Him in the temple,* <u>*sitting in the midst of the doctors, both hearing them, and asking them questions.*</u> *And all that heard Him were astonished at His understanding and answers. And when they saw him, they were amazed: and his mother said unto him, Son, why hast thou thus dealt with us? Behold, thy father and I have sought thee sorrowing. And He said unto them, how is it that ye sought me? Knew ye not that I must be about my Father's business?*

Luke 2, cont.

And they understood not the saying which He spake unto them. And He went down with them, and came to Nazareth, and was subject unto them: but his mother kept all these sayings in her heart. And OWYAZ increased in wisdom and stature, and in favor with AYAZ and man.

The Ruach of AYAZ taught OWYAZ!

From His early childhood OWYAZ was taught by the Spirit of AYAZ! OWYAZ makes that abundantly clear in His Psalms! OWYAZ was no ordinary child! OWYAZ was taught mysteries and insight from AYAZ twenty-four hours a day and seven days a week! OWYAZ was schooled in Yahuah's school of higher learning so that He would be ready, when it was His time to be put into Yahuah's furnace of affliction on the altar of earth! OWYAZ was anointed by AYAZ and appointed to fulfill His destiny as Israel's Passover Lamb! What happened to OWYAZ, after Yahushua's twelve year old Passover incident? The details of Yahushua's life as a teenager until the day He was immersed by John in the Yarden River remain a mystery in the Scriptures! However, the Scriptures as well as the Dead Sea Scrolls do record that as OWYAZ grew and matured, OWYAZ became more and more zealous for AYAZ even to the bursting point! OWYAZ may have followed the pattern of the prophets of AYAZ! When OWYAZ became a man and was considered a member of Israel, it is quite possible that OWYAZ retreated to the wilderness for a period of years away from Mary and Joseph to be taught by AYAZ! If OWYAZ did retreat to the wilderness to be completely <u>alone</u> with His Father, then that would explain the silence of the Scriptures for those years! There would have been no witnesses to write about that period of time unless OWYAZ wrote it Himself! Another scenario may have been that OWYAZ, the true Teacher of Righteous, taught and interacted with **others,** wherever He traveled, much like John the Immerser did with His followers in the wilderness! I believe that it would have been **extremely difficult**, if not impossible for OWYAZ to live without sharing His wisdom and understanding with others! **OWYAZ was bursting at the seams with His love and zeal for AYAZ**! How could OWYAZ possibly remain silent? If this scenario is correct, then that time in the life of OWYAZ may not have been a silent time at all! OWYAZ was definitely teaching His sheep somewhere!

Tears in a Bottle

When you make a comparison of the Davidic Psalms in the Scriptures with the Thanksgiving Hymns found at the Dead Sea, there is certainly no doubt that OWY₹Z is speaking in the first person in both! OWY₹Z is also definitely referred to in other Dead Sea Scrolls such as the War Scroll, the Community Rule, and the Damascus Document among <u>many</u> others! And there is no telling how much more fabulous information about OWY₹Z in the Dead Sea Scrolls has been suppressed from public view to this very day! Either way there's no question that OWY₹Z spent much private time with ₹Y₹Z in those years! Those would have been special times that His Father spent alone with OWY₹Z, teaching and preparing Him for the most important assignment in human history! This may be why there is a statement written by OWY₹Z in the Dead Sea Scrolls, which says that Joseph didn't know Me and My mother gave Me over to ₹Y₹Z! It's possible that Joseph had gone to his rest early in Yahushua's life and thus never knew OWY₹Z as a grown man! Or perhaps Mary and Joseph gave OWY₹Z over completely to ₹Y₹Z because they could no longer understand or cope with Yahushua's zealousness! At any rate this will remain a mystery for the time being, but one day soon, Israel will know everything because OWY₹Z will personally teach Israel just like ₹Y₹Z personally taught OWY₹Z! But one thing is overwhelmingly clear, OWY₹Z was extremely zealous for ₹Y₹Z from the very beginning of His life and He regarded ₹Y₹Z as His real father, even though Joseph was a very good man!

Psalms 71
[17]*Elohim, **You have taught me from my youth**; and to this day I declare Your wonders.*

Psalms 86
[11]*Teach me Your way, O ₹Y₹Z; let me walk in Your truth; unite my heart to fear Your Name.* [12]*I praise You, O ₹Y₹Z my Elohim, with all my heart, and I esteem Your name forever.* [13]*For Your kindness is great toward me, and You have delivered my being from the depths of the grave.* [14]*O Elohim, the proud have risen against me, and a band of dreaded men have sought my life, and have not set You before them.* [15]*But You, O ₹Y₹Z, are a compassionate El and showing favor, patient and great in kindness and truth.* [16]*Turn to me, and show favor to me! Give Your strength to Your servant, and save the <u>son of Your female servant</u>.*

Psalms 119

⁹⁷O how I love Your Torah! It is my study all day long. ⁹⁸Your commands make me wiser than my enemies; for it is ever before me. ⁹⁹I have more understanding than all my teachers, for Your witnesses are my study. **¹⁰⁰I understand <u>more than the aged</u> for I have observed Your orders. ¹⁰¹I have restrained my feet from every evil way, that I might guard Your word.** ¹⁰²I have not turned aside from Your right-rulings, for You Yourself have taught me. ¹⁰³How sweet to my taste has Your word been, more than honey to my mouth! ¹⁰⁴From Your orders I get understanding; therefore I have hated every false way. ¹⁰⁵Your word is a lamp to my feet and a light to my path. **¹⁰⁶I have <u>sworn</u>, and I confirm, to guard Your righteous right-rulings. ¹⁰⁷I have been afflicted very much;** O יהוה, revive me according to Your word. ¹⁰⁸Please accept the voluntary offerings of my mouth, O יהוה, and teach me Your right-rulings. ¹⁰⁹My life is in my hand continually, and **Your Torah I have not forgotten.** ¹¹⁰The wrong have laid a snare for me, but I have not strayed from Your orders.

Psalms 40

Then I said, "See, I have come; in the scroll of the Book it is pre-scribed for me. ⁸I have delighted to do Your pleasure, O my Elohim, And Your Torah is within my heart." ⁹I have proclaimed the good news of righteousness, in the great assembly; see, I do not restrain my lips, O יהוה, You know. ¹⁰I did not conceal Your righteousness within my heart; I have declared Your trustworthiness and Your deliverance; I did not hide Your kindness and Your truth From the great assembly. ¹¹Do not withhold Your compassion from me, O יהוה; let Your kindness and Your truth always watch over me. ¹²For evils without number have surrounded me; my crookednesses have overtaken me, and I have been unable to see; they became more than the hairs of my head; and my heart has failed me. ¹³Be pleased, O יהוה, to deliver me; O יהוה, hasten to help me! ¹⁴Let those who seek to destroy my life be ashamed and abashed altogether; let those who are desiring my evil be driven back and put to shame. ¹⁵Let those who say to me, "Aha, Aha!" be appalled at their own shame. ¹⁶Let all those who seek You Rejoice and be glad in You; let those who love Your deliverance always say, "יהוה be exalted!"

Dead Sea Scrolls
The Thanksgiving Psalms

Col 9

*These things I know through your understanding, **for You have opened my ears to wonderful mysteries** even though I am a vessel of clay and kneaded with water, a foundation of shame and a spring of filth, a melting pot of iniquity and a structure of sin, a spirit of error, perverted without understanding and terrified by righteous judgments.*

Col 12

***For <u>You have given me understanding</u> of the mysteries of Your wonder**, and in Your wondrous council You have confirmed; doing wonders before many for the sake of Your glory and making known Your mighty deeds to all living.*

Col 13

***Because [You] have exal[ted Yourself] in me, and <u>for sake of their guilt</u>**, You have hidden in me the spring of understanding and the counsel of truth.*

Col 16

***But You, O my Elohim, <u>have placed Your words in my mouth</u>** as showers of early rain, for all [who thirst] and as a spring of living waters.*

Col 17

***For You from my father have <u>known me from the womb</u> [You have set me apart and from the belly of] my mother** You have rendered good to me. From the breasts of she, who conceived me, Your compassion has been mine. And in the embrace of my nurse […] and from my youth, You have shined the insight of Your judgment on me. With a sure truth, You have supported me, and by Your Holy Spirit You have delighted me; even until this day […]. Your righteous chastisement is with my […] and the protection of Your peace delivers my soul. **With my steps is <u>abundant forgiveness and bountiful compassion</u>**, when You enter into judgment with me.*

Col 20

*And I, the **Instructor**, have known You, O my Elohim, by the spirit, which You gave me, and I have **listened faithfully** to Your wondrous council by Your Holy Spirit. You have opened within me knowledge in the mystery of Your insight, and a spring of [Your] strength […].*

Dead Sea Scrolls
The Thanksgiving Psalms

Col 17
With my steps is abundant forgiveness and bountiful compassion, when You enter into judgment with me. Until old age You shall provide for me, for __my father did not know me, and my mother abandoned me to You__. For you are a father to all the children of Your truth, and You rejoice over them as a loving mother over her nursing child. As a guardian with his embrace, you provide for all Your creatures.

Psalms 27
I sing, yea, I sing praises to ⱯYⱯZ. [7]Hear, O ⱯYⱯZ, when I cry with my voice! And show me favor, and answer me. [8]To my heart You have said, "__Seek My face.__" Your face, ⱯYⱯZ, I seek. [9]Do not hide Your face from me; do not turn Your servant away in displeasure; You have been my help; do not leave me nor forsake me, O Elohim of my deliverance. [10]__When my father and my mother have forsaken me, then ⱯYⱯZ does take me in__. [11]Teach me Your way, O ⱯYⱯZ,

Matthew, Mark, Luke, and John pick up the story of OWYⱯZ at His immersion by John at the river Yarden! OWYⱯZ was immersed in water by John! But afterwards ⱯYⱯZ would immerse OWYⱯZ in His furnace of affliction for the final 3½ years of His life! First OWYⱯZ was immersed by John with water, afterwards ⱯYⱯZ immersed OWYⱯZ in the fire of His furnace for the last 1260 days of Yahushua's life! So OWYⱯZ was immersed in water and fire, just as you will be, if you follow Yahushua's narrow Way! No other man has ever endured so much rejection, so much suffering, so many afflictions, so much betrayal, and so much humiliation as OWYⱯZ did! All the sufferings of Job plus all the afflictions of all the other servants of ⱯYⱯZ from every generation would __not__ __compare__ with what OWYⱯZ suffered during the last 3½ years of His life, when OWYⱯZ was in Yahuah's furnace of affliction!

Bless ⱯYⱯZ!
Bless ⱯYⱯZ!
Bless ⱯYⱯZ!

Tears in a Bottle

By the Mouth of Two or Three Witnesses

Matthew 18
*But if he will not hear thee, then take with thee one or two more, that in the **mouth of two or three witnesses every word may be established**.*

<u>Witness #1</u>

Matthew 3
And in those days Yohanan the Immerser came proclaiming in the wilderness of Yehudah, ²and saying, "Repent, for the reign of the heavens has come near!" ³For this is He who was spoken of by the prophet YeshaYahu, saying, "A voice of one crying in the wilderness, 'Prepare the way of ayaz, make His paths straight.' ⁴And Yohanan had a garment of camel's hair, and a leather girdle around his waist. And his food was locusts and wild honey. ⁵Then Yahrushalayim, and all Yehudah, and all the country around the Yarden went out to him, ⁶and they were immersed by him in the Yarden, confessing their sins. ⁷And seeing many of the Pharisees and Sadducees coming to his immersion, he said to them, "Brood of adders! Who has warned you to flee from the coming wrath? "Bear, therefore, fruits worthy of repentance, ⁹and do not think to say to yourselves, 'We have Abraham as father.' For I say to you that Elohim is able to raise up children to Abraham from these stones. ¹⁰"And the axe is already laid to the root of the trees. Every tree, then, which does not bear good fruit is cut down and thrown into the fire. ¹¹"I indeed immerse you in water unto repentance, but He who is coming after me is mightier than I, whose sandals I am not worthy to bear. He shall immerse you in the Set-apart Spirit and fire. ¹²"His winnowing fork is in His hand, and He shall thoroughly cleanse His threshing-floor, and gather His wheat into the storehouse, but the chaff He shall burn with unquenchable fire." ¹³Then OWYAZ came from Galil to Yohanan at the Yarden to be immersed by him. ¹⁴But Yohanan was hindering Him, saying, "I need to be immersed by You, and You come to me?" ¹⁵But OWYAZ answering, said to him, "Permit it now, for thus it is fitting for us to fill all righteousness." Then he permitted Him.

Matthew 3, cont.
[16]*And having been immersed, OWY3Z went up immediately from the water, and see, the heavens were opened, and He saw the Spirit of Elohim descending like a dove and coming upon Him,* [17]***and see, a voice out of the heavens, saying, "This is My Son, the Beloved, in whom I did delight."***

<u>**Witness #2**</u>

Mark 9
And after six days OWY3Z taketh with him Kepha, and James, and John, and leadeth them up into a high mountain apart by themselves: and He was transfigured before them. And his raiment became shining, exceeding white as snow; so as no fuller on earth can white them. And there appeared unto them EliYah with Moses: and they were talking with OWY3Z. And Kepha answered and said to OWY3Z, Rabbi, it is good for us to be here: and let us make three tabernacles; one for thee, and one for Moses, and one for EliYah. For he knew not what to say; for they were sore afraid. ***And there was a cloud that overshadowed them: and a voice came out of the cloud, saying,*** <u>***this is my beloved Son: Hear him***</u>*!*

<u>**Witness #3**</u>

John 12
And OWY3Z answered them, saying, the hour is come, that the Son of man should be glorified. Verily, verily, I say unto you, except a grain of wheat fall into the ground and die, it abideth alone: but if it die, it bringeth forth much fruit. ***He that loveth his life shall lose it; and he that hateth his life in this world shall keep it unto life eternal****. If any man serve me, let him follow me; and where I am, there shall also my servant be: if any man serve me, him will my Father honor. Now is my soul troubled; and what shall I say? Father, save me from this hour: but for this cause came I unto this hour. Father, glorify thy name.* <u>***Then came there a voice from heaven, saying, I have both glorified it, and will glorify it again***</u>*. The people therefore, that stood by, and heard it, said that it thundered: others said, an angel spake to him. OWY3Z answered and said, this voice came not because of me, but for your sakes. Now is the judgment of this world: now shall the prince of this world be cast out. And I, if I be lifted up from the earth, will draw all men unto me. This he said, signifying what death he should die.*

John 12, cont.
The people answered him, we have heard out of the law that the Messiah abideth for ever: and how sayest thou, the Son of man must be lifted up? Who is this Son of man? Then OWYƧZ *said unto them, Yet a little while is the light with you. Walk while ye have the light, lest darkness come upon you: for he that walketh in darkness knoweth not whither he goeth. While ye have light, believe in the light, that ye may be the* **children of light**. *These things spake* OWYƧZ, *and departed, and did hide himself from them. But though He had done so many miracles before them, yet* **they believed not** *on Him: That the saying of Isaiah the prophet might be fulfilled, which he spake,* ƧYƧZ, **who hath believed our report**? *And to whom hath the arm of* ƧYƧZ *been revealed? Therefore they could not believe, because that Isaiah said again,* **He hath blinded their eyes, and hardened their heart; that they should not see with their eyes, nor understand with their heart**, *and be converted, and I should heal them. These things said Isaiah, when he saw his glory, and spake of him.*

ƧYƧZ personally provided three witnesses from the heavens that OWYƧZ was in fact His anointed Son! ƧYƧZ was well pleased with OWYƧZ! That should have been **more than enough**, but it wasn't. Still the masses of Israel were completely blinded! They just didn't "**GET IT**"! But how can this be? Read on and discover the mystery surrounding Yahushua's tears!

Bless ƧYƧZ!
Bless ƧYƧZ!
Bless ƧYƧZ!
Bless ƧYƧZ!
Bless ƧYƧZ!

Chapter 2
Who Has Believed Our Report?

Dead Sea Scrolls
Thanksgiving Hymn Col 17 1QH

But as for Me, from ruin to desolation, from pain to agony, and from travails to torments my soul meditates on your wonders. In your mercy You have not rejected me. Time and time again my soul delights in the abundance of your compassion. I give an answer to those who would wipe me out, and reproof to those who would cast me down. I will condemn his verdict, but Your judgment I honor, for I know Your truth. I shall choose my judgment, and with my agony I am satisfied for I have waited upon Your mercy.

YeshaYahu (Isaiah) was a leader among the prophets of Israel. Isaiah's real name transliterated from Hebrew into English is YeshaYahu. No other prophet in the Tanach (Old Testament) was given so much wisdom and so much insight about future prophetic events as YeshaYahu! But perhaps the greatest message that YeshaYahu ever recorded was his report about Israel's future Messiah! YeshaYahu's report is recorded in YeshaYahu (Isaiah) 53 and the last two verses of YeshaYahu 52! YeshaYahu gave Israel the most reliable of testimonies about the exact nature of Yahushua's mission, His suffering, His purpose, and His ultimate victory! Most translators intentionally or perhaps unintentionally added additional confusion by poor translations of these verses! May ayaz rebuke them, if they knew better! Poor translations have obscured vital elements of YeshaYahu's message, which he was trying to communicate to all the future generations of Israel! Study and translate YeshaYahu's report for Yourself! **Look for Yahushua's tears!**

YeshaYahu, (Isaiah) 52
[14]As many were astonished at You – **so the <u>disfigurement</u> <u>beyond</u> <u>any</u> <u>man's</u>** and **<u>His form beyond the sons of men</u>** –[15]He shall likewise startle many nations. Sovereigns shut their mouths at Him, for **what had not been recounted to them they shall <u>see</u>**, and **what they had not heard they shall understand**.

YeshaYahu, (Isaiah) 53

<u>Who</u> <u>has</u> <u>believed</u> <u>our</u> <u>report</u>? *And to whom was the arm of* ᴣYᴣz *revealed?* [2]*For He grew up before Him as a tender plant, and as a root out of dry ground.* **He has no form or splendor that we should look upon Him, nor appearance that we should desire Him –** [3]**despised and rejected by men, a <u>man</u> <u>of</u> <u>pains</u> <u>and</u> <u>knowing</u> <u>sickness</u>. And as one from whom the <u>face</u> <u>is</u> <u>hidden</u>, being despised, and <u>we</u> <u>did</u> <u>not</u> <u>consider</u> Him.** [4]**<u>Truly</u>, <u>He</u> <u>has</u> <u>borne</u> <u>our</u> <u>sicknesses</u> and <u>carried</u> <u>our</u> <u>pains</u>. Yet <u>we</u> <u>reckoned</u> <u>Him</u> <u>stricken</u>, <u>smitten</u> <u>by</u> <u>Elohim</u>, and <u>afflicted</u>.** [5]*But He was pierced for our transgressions, He was crushed for our crookednesses. The chastisement for our peace was upon Him, and by His stripes we are healed.* [6]*We all, like sheep, went astray, each one of us has turned to his own way.* **And** ᴣYᴣz **has laid on Him the crookedness of us all**. [7]*He was oppressed and He was afflicted, but He did not open His mouth. He was led as a lamb to the slaughter, and as a sheep before its shearers is silent, but He did not open His mouth.* [8]*He was taken from prison and from judgment. And as for His generation, who considered that He shall be cut off from the land of the living?* **For the transgression of My people He was stricken.** [9]*And He was appointed a grave with the wrong, and with the rich at His death, because He had done no violence, nor was deceit in His mouth.*[1] [10]*But* ᴣYᴣz **was pleased to crush Him, He laid sickness on Him**, *that when He made Himself an offering for guilt, He would see a seed, He would prolong His days and the pleasure of* ᴣYᴣz *prosper in His hand.* [11]**He would see the result of the suffering of His life and be satisfied. Through His knowledge My righteous servant makes many righteous, and He bears their crookednesses.** [12]**Therefore I give Him a portion among the great, and He divides the spoil with the strong, because He poured out His being unto death, and He was counted with the transgressors, and He bore the sin of many, and made intercession for the transgressors**.

Because these two chapters are so important for every member of Israel to understand, I have recorded Isaiah 52 and 53 from the Blue Letter Bible, which is a free online translation service. The bolded words in parentheses are the expanded translations that I took the time to look up for additional clarity. Try the Blue Letter Bible for yourself, you'll like it! It will be a great "free" translation tool for you! Save it on your computer to "My Favorites".

Tears in a Bottle

YeshaYahu (Isaiah) 52

Isa 52:14 As many [07227] were astonied **(appalled, astonished, stuned)**[08074] at thee; his visage [04758] was so marred **(disfigurement of face)**, [04893] more than any man [0376], and his form **(appearance)**[08389] more than the sons [01121] of men [0120]:

Isa 52:15 So shall he **(startle)** sprinkle [05137] many [07227] nations [01471]; the kings [04428] <u>shall shut</u> [07092] <u>their mouths</u> [06310] at him: for [that] <u>which had not been told</u> [05608] <u>them</u> <u>shall they see</u> [07200]; and [that] <u>which they had not heard</u> [08085] <u>shall they consider</u> [0995].

YeshaYahu (Isaiah) 53

Isa 53:1 Who hath believed **(trusted)**[0539] our report **(message, instruction)**[08052]? And to whom is the arm **(mighty helper)**[02220] of ⱯYⱯZ **(Yahuah)**[03068] revealed **(to make known)**[01540]?

Isa 53:2 For he (OWYⱯZ))shall grow up [05927] before [06440] Him as a tender plant **(suckling, babe)**[03126], and as a root **(lowest part of a thing)**[08328] out of a dry [06723] **(wilderness)** ground **(country, territory)**[0776]: he hath no form **(appearance, countenance)**[08389] nor comeliness **(honor, splendor, majesty)**[01926]; and when we shall see [07200] him, [there is] no beauty **(fair appearance)**[04758] that we should desire **(delight greatly in)**[02530] him.

Isa 53:3 He is despised **(contemptible, scorned, disdained, considered vile)** [0959] and rejected **(made destitute by men, forsaken)**[02310] of men [0376]; a man [0376] of sorrows **(physical and mental pain)** [04341], and acquainted [03045] with grief **(sickness and diseases by first hand experience)** [02483]: and we hid as it were [04564] [our] faces [06440] from him; he was despised **(contemptible, scorned, disdained, considered vile)** [0959], and we esteemed **(prized, esteemed, to be equal to someone, to be taken for granted)** [02803] him not.

Isa 53:4 Surely [0403] He hath borne **(carried, endured)**[05375] our griefs **(sickness and diseases by first hand experience)**[02483], and carried [05445] our sorrows **(physical and mental pain)**[04341]: yet we did esteem [02803] him stricken **(stricken with disease, plagued with leprosy)**[05060], smitten **(send judgment upon, punished, smitten with disease)** [05221] of God [0430], and afflicted **(oppressed, humbled, be afflicted, be bowed down)** [06031].

YeshaYahu (Isaiah) 53, cont.

Isa 53:5 But He [was] wounded **(defiled, profaned, pierced, slain)** [02490] for our transgressions **(rebellion against Yahuah)** [06588], [he was] bruised **(crushed, humbled, made contrite, broken)**[01792] for our iniquities**(depravity, guilt, crimes)** [05771]: the chastisement **(discipline, correction, chastening)**[04148] of our peace **(completeness, soundness, health)**[07965] [was] upon him; and with his stripes **(wounds, hurts)**[02250] we are healed [07495].

Isa 53:6 All we like sheep [06629] have gone astray [08582]; we have turned [06437] every one [0376] to his own way **(way of living, way of worshiping)**[01870]; and ⟨Yahuah)[03068] hath laid [06293] on him the iniquity [05771] of us all.

Isa 53:7 He was oppressed **(harassed, distressed, hard pressed)**[05065], and He was afflicted **(oppressed, humbled, be afflicted, be bowed down)** [06031], yet He opened [06605] not his mouth [06310]: He is brought [02986] as a lamb [07716] to the slaughter [02874], and as a sheep [07353] before [06440] her shearers [01494] is dumb [0481], so He openeth [06605] not his mouth [06310].

Isa 53:8 He was taken [03947] from prison [06115] and from judgment [04941]: and who shall declare [07878] his generation [01755]? For he was cut off [01504] out of the land [0776] of the living [02416]: for the transgression **(rebellion against Yahuah)** [06588] of my people [05971] was He stricken **("nega" transliterated Hebrew word used to describe leprosy)** [05061] .

Isa 53:9 And he made [05414] his grave [06913] with the wicked [07563], and with the rich [06223] in his death [04194]; because he had done [06213] no violence [02555], neither [was any] deceit [04820] in his mouth [06310].

Isa 53:10 Yet it pleased [02654] ⟨Yahuah) [03068] to bruise [01792] him; he hath put [him] to grief **(made OWY⟨Z sick)** [02470]: when thou shalt make [07760] his soul [05315] an offering for sin [0817], He shall see [07200] [his] seed [02233], He shall prolong [0748] [his] days [03117], and the pleasure [02656] of ⟨Yahuah)[03068] shall prosper [06743] in his hand [03027].

Tears in a Bottle

YeshaYahu (Isaiah) 53, cont.

Isa 53:11 He shall see *[07200]* of the travail *[05999]* of his soul *[05315]*, *[and]* shall be satisfied *[07646]*: by his knowledge *[01847]* shall my righteous *[06662]* servant *[05650]* **justify** *[06663]* **many** *[07227]*; for he shall bear *[05445]* their iniquities *[05771]*.

Isa 53:12 Therefore will I divide *[02505]* him *[a portion]* with the great *[07227]*, and He shall divide *[02505]* the spoil *[07998]* with the strong *[06099]*; because He hath poured out *[06168]* his soul *[05315]* unto death *[04194]*: and He was numbered *[04487]* with the transgressors *[06586]*; and He bare *[05375]* the sin *[02399]* of many *[07227]*, and made intercession for the transgressors.

The Scripture passage below was used by ᕔᎽᗋ乙 to get my attention focused on the real OᗯᎽᗋ乙! As you read it for yourself, you will understand why I had to pull the string to find out more about the real OᗯᎽᗋ乙! This discovery ultimately led me to write *Tears in a Bottle*! When you read Luke 4 ask yourself this question. Why would those people in Nazareth be thinking, physician **you need to** heal yourself?

Physician Heal Yourself!

Luke 4
*And He came to Nazareth, where He had been brought up: and, as his custom was, He went into the synagogue on the Sabbath day, and stood up for to read. And there was delivered unto him the book of the prophet Isaiah. And when He had opened the book, He found the place where it was written, the Spirit of ᕔᎽᗋ乙 is upon me, because He hath anointed me to preach the gospel to the poor; He hath sent me to heal the brokenhearted, to preach deliverance to the captives, and recovering of sight to the blind, to set at liberty them that are bruised, to preach the acceptable year of ᕔᎽᗋ乙. And He closed the book, and He gave it again to the minister, and sat down. And the eyes of all them that were in the synagogue were fastened on him. And He began to say unto them, this day is this scripture fulfilled in your ears. And all bare him witness, and wondered at the gracious words which proceeded out of his mouth. And they said, is not this Joseph's son? And He said unto them, ye will surely say unto me this proverb, **physician, heal thyself: whatsoever we have heard done in Capernaum, do also here in thy country.***

We Thought He Had Leprosy!

One of the harshest realities that OWYƎZ experienced was the rejection, the disdain, and the contempt that He received from tens of thousands of the very people, who He came to save! Yahushua's rejection was so extreme that **thousands of people hid their faces from Him**! Why did they hide their faces? **They hid their faces because of Yahushua's repulsive physical appearance**! Multitudes of the sheep of Israel believed that OWYƎZ was **UNCLEAN** because He carried the marks of leprosy! By the end of His life, the appearance of Yahushua's face and body were marred more than any man's, even to the point that OWYƎZ **no longer even looked human**! Yahushua's severe disfigurement was caused by diseases, which He assimilated as He became the **sin bearer for all of Israel**! Without a doubt, the diseases that OWYƎZ carried included **leprosy**! As Yahushua's ministry progressed, OWYƎZ **literally** suffered the penalty for those people's rebellion **as well as ours** in His own mortal flesh! As OWYƎZ healed those sheep, He forgave their sins and took the penalty of their sins into His own body! OWYƎZ was **willing to do this** because of His boundless mercy, loving-kindness, and compassion towards Israel!

YeshaYahu 53:4 [4]*Truly, He has borne our sicknesses and carried our pains. Yet we reckoned Him stricken, **smitten** by Elohim, and afflicted.*

Jerome's Latin Vulgate Isaiah 53:4 *vere languores nostros ipse tulit et dolores nostros ipse portavit et nos putavimus eum quasi **leprosum** et percussum a Deo et humiliatum.*

We did esteem him stricken--judicially [LOWTH], namely, for *His* sins; whereas it was for *ours*. "**We thought Him to be a leper**" [JEROME, *Vulgate*], **leprosy** being the direct divine judgment for guilt.

Douay Rheims Bible Isaiah 53:4 *Surely He hath borne our infirmities and carried our sorrows: and we have thought Him as it were a **leper**, and as one struck by god (**should be** ƎYƎZ) and afflicted.*

Amplified Bible Isaiah 53:4 *Surely He has borne our griefs (sicknesses, weaknesses, and distresses) and carried our sorrows and pains [of punishment], yet we [ignorantly] considered Him stricken, smitten, and afflicted by god (**should be** ƎYƎZ) [as if with **leprosy**].*

Tears in a Bottle

The Orthodox Jewish Talmud records a story about a "Leper scholar". **Talmud Sanhedrin 98b.** "The Rabbis said: His name is 'the leper scholar,' as it is written, surely He hath borne our griefs, and carried our sorrows: yet we did esteem Him a leper, smitten of God **(should be ᴀYᴀZ)**, and afflicted."

The transliterated Hebrew words "naga" used in Isaiah 53:4 and "nega", used in Isaiah 53:8 are used almost exclusively in the Scriptures to describe the plague of leprosy! Nega (Neh'-gah, Strong's #5161) and naga (Na-gah', Strongs # 5060) are used repeatedly in the Scriptures in connection with being stricken or plagued with the **marks** of leprosy! Initially leprosy manifests itself as light spots or marks on the skin, which later evolve into severe festering boils of puss! Leprosy causes the hands and the feet to become severely clawed, knurled, and disfigured! Fingers and toes get shorter because of bone loss and they become **pitifully** distorted! The face and the eyes are severely deformed as the nose sinks into distorted facial muscles, which over time causes a multitude of eye abnormalities and eventual blindness! **Before the time of Constantine**, the followers of Yahushua's narrow Way were well aware that OWYᴀZ had leprosy! They knew that the appearance of OWYᴀZ was vile and repulsive! They also knew that by the end, OWYᴀZ didn't even look human anymore, just as YeshaYahu had reported! However, in the years, after Constantine, OWYᴀZ (renamed Ieous) was depicted by Rome as having perfect physical beauty and form! Of course, **that image is completely opposite from the TRUTH**, but that's still the image of ideal beauty that "Jesus" is depicted in today! But remember it's OWYᴀZ that I'm talking about, the anointed one of ᴀYᴀZ!

Is this the Messiah or should We look for another?
Why would John's disciples be so confused about Yahushua's identity? Hadn't John immersed OWYᴀZ in the Yarden River in the not too distant past? What had taken place that confused them so much? What had changed? The problem was that Yahushua's physical appearance had changed dramatically, since they had seen OWYᴀZ at His immersion! Now OWYᴀZ appeared to be cursed with leprosy and was nearly unrecognizable to them! Yahushua's appearance was progressively getting worse and worse, day by day! It was extremely difficult for them to understand what was happening to OWYᴀZ and **why** it was happening!

Tears in a Bottle

It confused them just as it would have confused us had we been there. Tens of thousands of the sheep of Israel were totally **offended** by Yahushua's dreadful physical appearance! So much so, that they hid their faces and the faces of their children from OWY∃Z! Others mocked Him **unmercifully**! Drunkards even sang songs about OWY∃Z in the streets! The sons of darkness mocked and joked about Yahushua's physical appearance **relentlessly**! As time went on, Yahushua's own friends and even His family became more and more estranged and alienated from Him! They kept their distance because they believed that OWY∃Z was **UNCLEAN**! Near the end OWY∃Z **became** a total outcast of society and **lived in dark places** away **from friends and family just like all the other lepers!**
But why did ∃Y∃Z determine to present His only begotten son in this fashion? ∃Y∃Z was looking for people back then just as He does today, **who do <u>not</u> judge by outward physical appearances! ∃Y∃Z looks for people, who judge the right way by using Yahuah's insight to measure the inner worth of someone or something**! In Yahushua's case the sheep should have judged OWY∃Z by what He said and the miracles that He did!

Luke 7
*Then OWY∃Z answering said unto them, go your way, and tell John what things ye have seen and heard; how that the blind see, the lame walk, the lepers are cleansed, the deaf hear, the dead are raised, to the poor the good news is preached. And blessed is he, **whosoever shall not be offended in me (those <u>not</u> offended by the dreadful appearance of OWY∃Z).***

The signs and wonders should have been **more than enough**, if those blinded sheep had not been so offended by Yahushua's terrible physical appearance! What do you think? Are you offended? True love is much deeper than outward appearances, is it not? Do you believe YeshaYahu's report? OWY∃Z suffered so much more than we have been led to believe by the false shepherds! It's just mind boggling to me that such lies have been perpetuated for so long! Why haven't they told us these things? Aren't they supposed to be able to rightly interpret the Scriptures? The false shepherds are blinded just like the sheep, who follow them. **The blind still lead the blind!**

Matthew 15:14 Let them alone: they be blind leaders of the blind. And if the blind lead the blind, both shall fall into the ditch.

Tears in a Bottle

Shall we look for another?

Luke 7

And this rumor of him went forth throughout all Judaea, and throughout all the region round about. And the disciples of John shewed him of all these things. And John calling unto him two of his disciples sent them to OWY︎︎︎ᴚⱿ︎, *saying, art thou he that should come? Or look we for another? When the men were come unto him, they said, John the Baptist hath sent us unto thee,* **saying, art thou he that should come or look we for another?** *And in that same hour He cured many of their infirmities and plagues, and of evil spirits; and unto many that were blind He gave sight. Then* OWY︎︎︎ᴚⱿ *answering said unto them, go your way, and tell John what things ye have seen and heard; how that the blind see, the lame walk, the lepers are cleansed, the deaf hear, the dead are raised, to the poor the gospel is preached. And blessed is he, whosoever* **shall not be offended** *in Me.*

In the familiar story below, please pay particular attention to the reaction of the town's people, when they came out to **see** OWY︎︎︎ᴚⱿ, after He had healed the man possessed with the unclean spirits! What was it about OWY︎︎︎ᴚⱿ that **terrified** those people so much that they asked OWY︎︎︎ᴚⱿ to immediately leave their coasts! **Of course, it was Yahushua's leprous appearance!**

Please leave our coasts!

Matthew 8

And when He was come to the other side into the country of the Gergesenes, there met him two possessed with devils, coming out of the tombs, exceeding fierce, so that no man might pass by that way. And, behold, they cried out, saying, What have we to do with thee, OWY︎︎︎ᴚⱿ, *thou Son of Elohim? Art thou come hither to torment us before the time? And there was a good way off from them a herd of many swine feeding. So the devils besought him, saying, if thou cast us out, suffer us to go away into the herd of swine. And He said unto them, Go. And when they were come out, they went into the herd of swine: and, behold, the whole herd of swine ran violently down a steep place into the sea, and perished in the waters. And they that kept them fled, and went their ways into the city, and told every thing, and what was befallen to the possessed of the devils. And, behold, the whole city came out to meet* OWY︎︎︎ᴚⱿ: ***and when they* saw *him,* they besought him that He would depart out of their coasts.**

see Matt. 8:17

Matthew 8, cont.
They were taken with great fear: *and He went up into the ship, and returned back again.*

The Alabaster Jar

The story below is a very touching story, but the story is even more special, when you consider it in light of Yahushua's leprous condition! Mary, who was the sister of Lazarus, was so overcome with love and **compassion** for OWYヨ‹, that she poured the expensive ointment on Yahushua's head, feet, and body! Mary **desperately** wanted to sooth the pain and misery of Yahushua's lesions and boils with the expensive spikenard ointment! Mary didn't care how much the ointment cost! She applied the soothing ointment to Yahuahua's sores and lesions! Mary wiped Yahushua's feet with her hair and kissed His feet repeatedly! Kissing the feet of a leper would be unheard of in all the Land of Israel under normal conditions, but Mary loved OWYヨ‹ so much that outward appearances **did not matter** to her at all! She was so thankful for Yahushua that **she didn't care what Yahushua's outward appearance or His feet looked like**! Mary didn't care, if OWYヨ‹ looked "unclean"! All she knew was that she loved OWYヨ‹ with all her heart! Mary wept profusely, when she saw the boils and lesions on Yahushua's face, hands, legs, and feet! **She couldn't stop crying because she knew that OWYヨ‹ was suffering horribly in His own body for her sins and the sins of others**! When we see OWYヨ‹, we won't be able to stop crying either!

Matthew 26
Now when OWYヨ‹ *was in Bethany, in the house of* **Simon the leper***, There came unto him a woman having an alabaster box of very precious ointment, and poured it on his head, as he sat at meat. But when his disciples saw it, they had indignation, saying, to what purpose is this waste? For this ointment might have been sold for much, and given to the poor. When* OWYヨ‹ *understood it, He said unto them, why trouble ye the woman? For she hath wrought a good work upon Me. For ye have the poor always with you; but Me ye have not always. For in that she hath poured this ointment on my body, she did it for my burial.*

Tears in a Bottle

What is Spikenard?

Spikenard is an aromatic plant whose root is used in the preparation of medicinal ointments for curing bruises; the very smell of the plant was said to destroy fleas. Spikenard (also nard and muskroot) is a flowering plant of the Valerian family. The plant grows to about 1m in height and has pink, bell-shaped flowers. Spikenard rhizomes (underground stems) can be crushed and distilled into an intensely aromatic, amber-colored essential oil. Nard oil is used as a perfume, an incense, a sedative, and an herbal medicine said to fight insomnia, flatulence, birth difficulties, and other minor ailments.

Mark 14

*And being in Bethany in the house of **Simon the leper**, as He sat at meat, there came a woman having an alabaster box of ointment of spikenard very precious; and she brake the box, and poured it on His head. And there were some that had indignation within themselves, and said, why was this waste of the ointment made? For it might have been sold for more than three hundred pence, and have been given to the poor. And they murmured against her. And* OWY_{AL} *said, let her alone; why trouble ye her? She hath wrought a good work on Me. For ye have the poor with you always, and whensoever ye will ye may do them good: but Me ye have not always. She hath done what she could: she is come aforehand to anoint my body to the burying. Verily I say unto you, wheresoever this good news shall be preached throughout the whole world, this also that she hath done shall be spoken of for a memorial of her.*

Luke 7

*And **one of the Pharisees** desired him that he would eat with him. And He went into the Pharisee's house, and sat down to meat. And, behold, a woman in the city, which was a sinner, when she knew that* OWYAL *sat at meat in the Pharisee's house, brought an alabaster box of ointment, and **stood at His feet behind him weeping, and began to wash His feet with tears, and did wipe them with the hairs of her head, and kissed His feet, and anointed them with the ointment**. Now when the Pharisee which had bidden Him saw it, He spake within himself, saying, This man, if He were a prophet, would have known who and what manner of woman this is that toucheth Him: for she is a sinner. And* OWYAL *answering said unto Him, Simon, I have somewhat to say unto thee.*

Tears in a Bottle

Luke 7, cont.
And He saith, Master, say on. There was a certain creditor which had two debtors: the one owed five hundred pence, and the other fifty. And when they had nothing to pay, He frankly forgave them both. Tell Me therefore, which of them will love him most? Simon answered and said, I suppose that he, to whom he forgave most. And He said unto him, thou hast rightly judged. And He turned to the woman, and said unto Simon, seest thou this woman? I entered into thine house, thou gavest Me no water for my feet: but she hath washed my feet with tears, and wiped them with the hairs of her head. Thou gavest Me no kiss: but this woman since the time I came in hath not ceased to kiss my feet. My head with oil thou didst not anoint: but this woman hath anointed my feet with ointment. Wherefore I say unto thee, her sins, which are many, are forgiven; for she loved much: but to whom little is forgiven, the same loveth little. And He said unto her, **thy sins are forgiven**. And they that sat at meat with him began to say within themselves, who is this that forgiveth sins also? And He said to the woman, thy faith hath saved thee; go in peace.

John 12
Then OWYƎⱿ six days before the Passover came to Bethany, where Lazarus was which had been dead, whom He raised from the dead. There they made him a supper; and Martha served: but Lazarus was one of them that sat at the table with him. **Then took Mary a pound of ointment of spikenard, very costly, and anointed the feet of OWYƎⱿ, and wiped His feet with her hair: and the house was filled with the odor of the ointment.** Then saith one of his disciples, Judas Iscariot, Simon's son, which should betray him, why was not this ointment sold for three hundred pence, and given to the poor? This he said, not that he cared for the poor; but because he was a thief, and had the bag, and bare what was put therein. Then said OWYƎⱿ, let her alone: against the day of my burying hath she kept this. For the poor always ye have with you; but Me ye have not always.

Psalms 22 is a very well know Messianic passage, but it takes on knew meaning, **when you know the truth**!

Tears in a Bottle

I am more worm than Man!

Psalms 22

My El, my El, why hast thou forsaken me? ꜩꞀꜩꙀ *art thou so far from helping me and from the words of my roaring? O my Elohim I cry in the daytime, but thou hearest not and in the night season and am not silent. But thou art holy, O thou that inhabitest the praises of Israel. Our fathers trusted in thee: they trusted, and thou didst deliver them. They cried unto thee, and were delivered: they trusted in thee, and were not confounded.* **But I am a worm (or now more worm than man), and no man; a reproach of men, and despised of the people.** *All they that* <u>**see me laugh me to scorn**</u>**: they shoot out the lip, they shake the head saying, He trusted on** ꜩꞀꜩꙀ **that He would deliver him: let him deliver him, seeing He delighted in him. But thou art He that took me out of the womb**: *thou didst make me hope when I was upon my mother's breasts.* **I was cast upon thee from the womb: thou art my El from** <u>**my**</u> <u>**mother's belly**</u>. *Be not far from me; for trouble is near; for there is none to help. Many bulls have compassed me: strong bulls of Bashan have beset me round. They gaped upon me with their mouths, as a ravening and a roaring lion.* **I am poured out like water, and all my bones are out of joint: my heart is like wax; it is melted in the midst of my bowels. My strength is dried up like a potsherd; and my tongue cleaveth to my jaws;** *and thou hast brought me into the dust of death. For dogs have compassed me: the assembly of the wicked have enclosed Me: they pierced my hands and my feet.* **(alternate translations: they have torn and plucked as a Lion at my hands and feet or they have laid snares at my hands and feet)** *I may tell all my bones: they look and stare upon me. They part my garments among them, and cast lots upon my vesture. But be not thou far from me, O* ꜩꞀꜩꙀ*: O my strength, haste thee to help me. Deliver my soul from the sword; my darling from the power of the dog. Save me from the lion's mouth: for thou hast heard me from the horns of the unicorns.* **I will declare thy name unto my brethren: in the midst of the congregation will I praise thee**. *Ye that fear* ꜩꞀꜩꙀ*, praise him; all ye the seed of Jacob, glorify him; and fear him, all ye the seed of Israel.* **For He hath not despised nor abhorred the affliction of the afflicted; neither hath He hid his face from him; but when He cried unto him, He heard.** *My praise shall be of thee in the great congregation: I will pay my vows before them that fear him.*

HelleluYah! Praise Yah!

Psalms 148

Praise Yah! Praise 𐤀𐤉𐤄𐤆 *from the heavens, Praise Him in the heights! [2]Praise Him, all His messengers; Praise Him, all His hosts! [3]Praise Him, sun and moon; Praise Him, all you stars of light! [4]Praise Him, heavens of heavens, and you waters above the heavens! [5]Let them praise the Name of* 𐤀𐤉𐤄𐤆, *For He commanded and they were created. [6]And He established them forever and ever, He gave a law and they pass not beyond. [7]Praise* 𐤀𐤉𐤄𐤆 *from the earth, You great sea creatures and all the depths, [8]fire and hail, snow and clouds, stormy wind that does His word, [9]the mountains and all hills, fruit tree and all cedars, [10]wild beasts and all cattle, creeping creatures and flying birds, [11]sovereigns of the earth and all peoples, rulers and all judges of the earth, [12]both young men and maidens, old men and children. [13]Let them praise the Name of* 𐤀𐤉𐤄𐤆, *for His Name alone is exalted, His splendor is above the earth and heavens. [14]He also lifts up the horn of His people, the praise of all His kind ones; of the children of Yisra'el, a people near to Him. Praise Yah!*

Psalms 149

Praise Yah! Sing to 𐤀𐤉𐤄𐤆 *a new song, His praise in an assembly of kind ones. [2]Let Yisra'el rejoice in their Maker; Let the children of Tsiyon exult in their Sovereign. [3]Let them praise His Name in a dance; Let them sing praises to Him with the tambourine and lyre. [4]For* 𐤀𐤉𐤄𐤆 *takes pleasure in His people; He embellishes the meek ones with deliverance. [5]Let the kind ones exult in esteem; Let them sing aloud on their beds. [6]Let the exaltation of El be in their mouth, and a two-edged sword in their hand, [7]To execute vengeance on the gentiles, punishments on the peoples; [8]To bind their sovereigns with chains, and their nobles with iron bands; [9]To execute on them the written right-ruling;a splendor it is for all His kind ones. Praise Yah*

Psalms 150

Praise Yah! Praise El in His set-apart place; Praise Him in His mighty expanse! [2]Praise Him for His mighty acts; Praise Him according to His excellent greatness! [3]Praise Him with the blowing of the ram's horn; Praise Him with the harp and lyre! [4]Praise Him with tambourine and dance; Praise Him with stringed instruments and flutes! [5]Praise Him with sounding cymbals; Praise Him with resounding cymbals! [6]Let all that have breath praise Yah. Praise Yah!

Tears in a Bottle

My Loins are filled with a Loathsome Disease!

Psalms 38

O ΑΥΑΖ, rebuke me not in thy wrath: neither chasten me in thy hot displeasure. **For thine arrows stick fast in me, and thy hand presseth me sore. There is no soundness in my flesh because of thine anger; neither is there any rest in my bones because of my sin.** *For mine iniquities are gone over mine head: as a heavy burden they are too heavy for me.* **My wounds stink and are corrupt because of my foolishness. I am troubled; I am bowed down greatly; I go mourning all the day long. For my loins are filled with a loathsome disease: and there is no soundness in my flesh. I am feeble and sore broken: I have roared by reason of the disquietness of my heart. ΑΥΑΖ, all my desire is before thee; and my groaning is not hid from thee. My heart panteth, my strength faileth me: as for the light of mine eyes, it also is gone from me. My lovers and my friends stand aloof from my sore; and my kinsmen stand afar off. They also that seek after my life lay snares for me: and they that seek my hurt speak mischievous things, and imagine deceits all the day long. But I, as a deaf man, heard not; and I was as a dumb man that openeth not his mouth. Thus I was as a man that heareth not, and in whose mouth are no reproofs. For in thee, O ΑΥΑΖ, do I hope**: *thou wilt hear, O ΑΥΑΖ my Elohim. For I said, hear me, lest otherwise they should rejoice over me: when my foot slippeth, they magnify themselves against me.* **For I am ready to halt, and my sorrow is continually before me.** *For I will declare mine iniquity;* **I will be sorry for my sin (the sins of others that OWYΑΖ carried).** *But mine enemies are lively, and they are strong: and they that hate me wrongfully are multiplied. They also that render evil for good are mine adversaries; because I follow the thing that good is. Forsake me not, O ΑΥΑΖ: O my Elohim, be not far from me. make haste to help me, O ΑΥΑΖ my salvation.*

OWYΑΖ was Yahuah's sin offering for all the overcomers of Israel! OWYΑΖ took on the sins of others and He suffered the penalty for the sins and rebellions of others in His own flesh in the form of wasting diseases! The magnitude of Yahushua's suffering just boggles my mind! OWYΑΖ knew that by His suffering, many brothers and sisters would be accepted into the kingdom of ΑΥΑΖ! I am not worthy to retell the story of so great a Deliverer as Israel's OWYΑΖ!

Chapter 3
Put My Tears into Your Bottle!

[5]All day long they twist my words; all their thoughts are against Me for evil. [6]They stir up strife, they hide, they watch my steps, as they lie in wait for my life. [7]Because of wickedness, cast them out. Put down the peoples in displeasure, O Elohim! [8]You have counted my wanderings; You put my tears into Your bottle; are they not in Your book?...Tehillim (Psalms) 56

When OWYƎZ sojourned on earth as Israel's Passover Lamb, He suffered terribly! **For nearly 1,700 years the real magnitude of Yahushua's suffering has been suppressed and forgotten by almost everyone on the planet! As a result, the real magnitude and the real nature of Yahushua's suffering have been totally lost and underestimated!** The real nature of Yahushua's suffering has been suppressed, since the time of Constantine! Constantine changed the image of OWYƎZ into the Greek image of physical perfection and perfect beauty! Today Constantine's image of physical perfection still dominates Christian religious thought! When the sheep discuss Yahushua's suffering, the focus is always on Yahushua's sacrifice on the Passover Tree. Yahushua's death on the tree **was horrible**, but it does **not** compare with the continuous pain and the agonizing misery that OWYƎZ experienced each and every day as His ministry progressed. OWYƎZ faced unparalleled struggles, rejections, persecutions, and afflictions all simultaneously during His extremely intense 3½ ministry! Early in His ministry, OWYƎZ became **Target #1** for the wrath of the prevailing religious authorities! The religious leaders led by "the Wicked Priest" Caiaphas, **continuously** conspired to kill OWYƎZ! Their scheming was relentless! OWYƎZ stated that those religious leaders were continuously looking to trap Him! They would often say the words **"Aha, Aha"**, when they believed they had OWYƎZ! Even Yahushua's family, friends, and close companions became more and more distant as His physical condition worsened with the passing of each day! The same disciples, who had initially flocked to hear OWYƎZ, **abandoned Him** as time went on, when His physical condition worsened and His teaching became more and more intense!

Tears in a Bottle

During His ministry, even Yahushua's own twelve disciples often quarreled because of their jealously toward each other and their lack of understanding. All these things alone would have been enough to crush anyone, but Yahushua's suffering got much, much worse! OWY useful assimilated leprosy as well as other terrible wasting diseases! **He was in constant pain and could not get any rest**! OWY useful assumed the full penalty for our sins and transgressions in His own flesh! OWY useful never sinned, but He **literally** took on the sins of others **willingly**! The weight of those sins was extremely difficult for OWY useful to carry! Sin in all its forms was completely repulsive and foreign to OWY useful! OWY useful literally carried all the sins of Israel and the weight of that sin vexed His spirit! It just broke Yahushua's heart!

Leprosy has been known, since ancient times, as "the living death"! Our precious OWY useful carried the full weight of that disease in His own flesh thanks to our sins and rebellions! Leprosy horribly affects the skin, face, hands, feet, and eyes as it attacks the central nervous system. OWY useful spoke of the emaciated condition of His body, which resulted from His infirmities and His severe fasting! He spoke of the bad smell coming from His wounds and the worms living in His festering flesh! He spoke repeatedly about His bones being disjointed in both the Davidic Psalms and the Thanksgiving Hymns of Dead Sea Scrolls! This was all **before** OWY useful **hung on the Passover Tree**! OWY useful lamented about His arm being dislocated from His shoulder, which prevented Him from swinging His arm as He tried to walk about. And He spoke repeatedly about his tongue sticking to the roof of His mouth, which made talking increasingly difficult! Leprosy dramatically alters the facial muscles, which made Yahushua's facial appearance appear extremely disfigured and even grotesque to the observer. YeshaYahu recorded in YeshaYahu (Isaiah 52) that OWY useful **did** **not** even look human anymore and **He could no longer see well**! Over time the facial damage resulting from His leprosy, had a profound impact on Yahushua's ability to communicate! By the end of His ministry it was very difficult for OWY useful to speak! As He approached the end, OWY useful could no longer physically minister the way He had earlier in His ministry because walking, standing, and speaking were incredibably painful for OWY useful! By the end OWY useful was bowed over very low and groaned out loud from the pain and burning. He trembled like an old man and stumbled, when He walked, even though OWY useful was only thirty-three years old.

Tears in a Bottle

At the end Yahushua's physical condition made it so difficult to speak that Pilate misinterpreted Yahushua's dumbness as a refusal to defend Himself! Yahuah's Ruach Ha Qodesh has opened my eyes to see the real OWY3Z! When I saw and understood the real OWY3Z, **the truth broke my heart**! I understand why Mary, the sister of Lazarus, was so overcome with emotion, when she saw Yahushua's condition! Mary empathized with Yahushua's pain and suffering! Mary did all that she could for OWY3Z, when she poured the Spikenard on Yahushua's body! Mary tried her best to sooth Yahushua's pain, which was caused by the plagues OWY3Z received **because of my sins and the sins of others**! My purpose for writing *Tears in a Bottle* is to retell the story of the real OWY3Z to all the hungry sheep of Israel! I hope that *Tears in a Bottle* will help you realize just how much OWY3Z really loves you! OWY3Z was willing to suffer all these things for the overcomers of Israel! The whole world desperately needs to understand **how and why OWY3Z suffered** and **how He overcame**! **It's imperative that the hungry sheep of Israel follow Yahushua's pattern for overcoming in their own lives**! Follow Yahushua's example for overcoming, **when you are placed** in Yahuah's furnace of affliction! Please, please, please don't let a single one of Yahushua's tears be wasted in your life!

You have made Me an abomination to them!
Psalms 88
O 𐤉𐤄𐤅𐤄, Elohim of my deliverance, **by day I have <u>cried out</u>**, in the night also before You, [2]*let my prayer come before You, incline Your ear to my <u>cry</u>*. [3]*For my being is **filled with evils, and my life draws near to the grave**. [4]**I have been reckoned among those who go down to the pit; I have become like a man who has no strength**, [5]Released among the dead, like slain ones lying in the grave, whom You have remembered no more, and who have been cut off from Your hand. [6]You have put me in the lowest pit, in dark places, in the depths. [7]Your wrath has rested heavily upon me, and **You have afflicted me with all Your breakers**. Selah. [8]<u>**You have put away my friends far from me; You have made me an abomination to them; I am shut in**</u> and do not go out; [9]<u>my eye grows dim</u> because of affliction*. 𐤉𐤄𐤅𐤄, *I have called upon You, all day long; I have stretched out my hands to You. [10]Would You work wonders for the dead? Would the dead rise to praise You? Selah. [11]Is Your kindness declared in the grave?*

Psalms 88, cont.
Your trustworthiness in the place of destruction? ^{12}*Are Your wonders known in the dark? And Your righteousness in the land of no remembrance?* ^{13}*But I, unto You I have cried, O* יהוה*, and in the morning my prayer comes before You.* ^{14}יהוה *why do You reject me? Why do You hide Your face from me?* ^{15}*I am afflicted and dying from childhood;* **I have borne frightening matters from You; I am in despair.** ^{16}**Your fierce wrath has gone over me**; *Your onslaughts have cut me off.* ^{17}*They surrounded me like water all day long; they close in upon me altogether.* ^{18}**You have put loved one and companion far from me, <u>darkness is my close friend</u>**!

All those who <u>see</u> Me mock Me!

Psalms 22
My El, My El, why have You forsaken Me – Far from saving Me, far from the words of **My <u>groaning</u>**? ^{2}*O My Elohim, I call by day, but You do not answer; and by night, but I find* **<u>no rest</u>**. ^{3}*Yet You are set-apart, enthroned on the praises of Yisra'el.* ^{4}*Our fathers trusted in You; they trusted, and You delivered them.* ^{5}*They cried to You, and were delivered; they trusted in You, and were not ashamed.* ^{6}**But <u>I am a worm</u>, <u>and no man</u>; a reproach of men, and despised by the people.** ^{7}**All <u>those who see Me mock Me</u>; They shoot out the lip, they shake the head, saying,** ^{8}**"He trusted in** יהוה**, let Him rescue Him; Let Him deliver Him, seeing He has delighted in Him!"** ^{9}*For You are the One who took Me out of the womb;* **causing Me to trust while on My mother's breasts.** ^{10}**I was cast upon You from birth. From My mother's belly You have been My El.** ^{11}*Do not be far from Me, for distress is near; for there is none to help.* ^{12}*Many bulls have surrounded Me; strong ones of Bashan have encircled Me.* ^{13}**They have opened their mouths against Me, as a raging and roaring lion.** ^{14}*I have been poured out like water,* **and all My bones have been spread apart**; *my heart has become like wax; it has melted in the midst of My inward parts.* ^{15}*My strength is dried like a potsherd,* **and My tongue is cleaving to My jaws**; *and to the dust of death You are appointing Me.* ^{16}*For dogs have surrounded Me; a crowd of evil ones have encircled Me, piercing my hands and my feet;* ^{17}*I count all my bones. They look,* **they stare at Me. (the Passover tree)** ^{18}*They divide my garments among them, and for my raiment they cast lots.* **(the Passover tree)** ^{19}*But You, O* יהוה*, do not be far off; O My Strength, hasten to help Me!* ^{20}*Deliver My life from the sword, my only life from the power of the dog.*

Tears in a Bottle

Psalms 22, cont.
²⁴For <u>He has not despised nor hated the affliction of the afflicted</u>; **nor has He hidden His face from Him**; *but when He cried to Him, He heard.* ²⁵*From You is My praise in the great assembly;* **I pay My vows**, *before those who fear Him.* ²⁶*The meek ones do eat and are satisfied; let those who seek Him praise* **ayaz**.

In my distress I called upon ayaz!

Psalms 17
Hear righteousness, **ayaz**, *listen to* **my** <u>cry</u>; *give ear to my prayer, from lips without deceit.* ²*Let my right-ruling go out from Your presence; let Your eyes see what is straight.* ³*You have examined my heart; You have visited me in the night;* **You have** <u>tried</u> **me** – *You find I have not schemed; my mouth would not transgress.* ⁴*As for the deeds of men – by the word of Your lips, I have kept myself from the paths of the destroyer.* ⁵*My steps have held fast to Your paths, my feet have not slipped.* ⁶*I have called upon You, for You answer me, O El; incline Your ear to me, hear my speech.* ⁷*Let Your kindness be distinguished, You who save by Your right hand those who take refuge from those who rise up.* ⁸*Guard me as the apple **(pupil)** of Your eye.* **Hide me under the shadow of Your wings,** ⁹**from the face of the wrong, who ravage me, from my deadly enemies who surround me.** ¹⁰**They are enclosed in their own fat, they speak proudly with their mouths,** ¹¹*they have now surrounded us in our steps, they set their eyes to cast us to the ground,* ¹²*Like a lion who is eager to tear his prey, and as a young lion crouching in cover.* ¹³*Arise, O* **ayaz**, *confront him, cause him to bend; deliver my being from the wrong by Your sword,* ¹⁴*from men by Your hand, O* **ayaz**, *from men of the world whose portion is in this life, and You fill their bellies with Your treasure, they are satisfied with children, and shall leave their riches to their babes.* ¹⁵*As for me, let Me see Your face in righteousness; I am satisfied to see Your appearance, when I awake.*

Psalms 18
I love You, O **ayaz**, *my strength.* ²**ayaz** *is my rock and my stronghold and my deliverer; my El is my rock, I take refuge in Him; my shield and the horn of my deliverance, my high tower.* ³*I call upon* **ayaz**, *the One to be praised, and I am saved from my enemies.* ⁴*The cords of death surrounded me, and the floods of Beliya'al made me afraid.* ⁵*The cords of the grave were all around me; the snares of death were before me.*

Tears in a Bottle

Those who <u>see</u> Me outside flee from Me!

Psalms 31

In You, O 𐤉𐤄𐤅𐤄, I have taken refuge; let me never be ashamed; deliver me in Your righteousness. [2]Incline Your ear to me, deliver me speedily; be a rock of refuge to me, a house of defense to save me. [3]For You are my rock and my stronghold; for Your Name's sake lead me and guide me. [4]Bring me out of the **net which they have hidden for me**, for You are my stronghold. [5]Into Your hand I commit my spirit; You have redeemed me, O 𐤉𐤄𐤅𐤄 El of truth. [6]I have hated those who observe lying vanities; but I trust in 𐤉𐤄𐤅𐤄. [7]I exult and rejoice in Your kindness, **for You have seen my affliction; You have known the distresses of my life**, [8]and You have not shut me up into the hand of the enemy. You have set my feet in a large place. [9]Show me favor, O 𐤉𐤄𐤅𐤄, **for I am in distress; my eye, my being and my body have become old with grief! [10]For my life is consumed in sorrow, and my years in sighing; my strength fails because of my crookedness, and my bones have become old. [11]I am a reproach among all my adversaries, but most of all among my neighbors, and a dread to my friends; <u>those who see me outside flee from me</u>. [12]I have been forgotten like someone dead from the heart; I have been like a missing vessel. [13]For I hear the evil report of many; fear is from all around; when they take counsel together against me, <u>they plot to take away my life</u>. [14]But I, <u>I have put my trust in You</u>, O 𐤉𐤄𐤅𐤄; I have said, "You are my Elohim." [15]<u>My times are in Your hand</u>**; deliver me from the hand of my enemies, and from those who pursue me. [16]Make Your face shine upon Your servant; save me in Your kindness. [17]Do not let me be ashamed, O 𐤉𐤄𐤅𐤄, for I have called upon You; let the wrong be ashamed; let them be silenced in the grave. [18]Let lips of falsehood be stilled, which speak recklessly against the righteous, with pride and scorn. [19]**How great is Your goodness, which You have laid up for those fearing You, which You have prepared for those taking refuge in You In the sight of the sons of men!** [20]In the secrecy of Your presence You shall hide them from the plots of man; You shelter them in a booth from the strife of tongues. [21]Blessed be 𐤉𐤄𐤅𐤄, for He has made marvelous His kindness to me in a strong city! [22]And I, I have said in my haste, "I am cut off from before Your eyes," yet You heard the voice of my prayers when I cried out to You. [23]Love 𐤉𐤄𐤅𐤄, all you His kind ones!

Tears in a Bottle

They say, "Aha, Aha!"

Psalms 35

O 𐤉𐤄𐤅𐤄, *strive with those who strive with me;* **fight against those who fight against me.** [2]*Take hold of shield and armor, and rise for my help.* [3]*And draw out spear and lance, to meet those who pursue me. Say to my life, "I am your deliverance."* [4]**Let those be ashamed and blush who seek my life;** *let those be turned back and abashed,* **who plot evil to me.** [5]*Let them be as chaff before the wind with a messenger of* 𐤉𐤄𐤅𐤄 *driving on.* [6]*Let their way be dark and slippery, with a messenger of* 𐤉𐤄𐤅𐤄 *pursuing them.* [7]**For without cause they hid their net for me; without cause they dug a pit for my life.** [8]*Let ruin come upon him unawares, and let his net that he hid catch himself; let him fall in it, into ruin.* [9]*But let my own being exult in* 𐤉𐤄𐤅𐤄; *let it rejoice in His deliverance.* [10]*Let all my bones say, "*𐤉𐤄𐤅𐤄, *who is like You, delivering the poor from one stronger than he, and the poor and the needy from him who robs him?"* [11]*Ruthless witnesses rise up; they ask me that which I knew not.* [12]**They reward me evil for good, bereaving my life.** [13]**But I, when they were sick, I put on sackcloth; I humbled my being with fastings; and my prayer would return to my own bosom.** [14]**I walked about as though he were my friend or brother; I bowed down mourning, as one mourning for a mother.** [15]**But they rejoiced at my stumbling and gathered together; the smiters gathered against me, and I did not know it; they tore in pieces without ceasing,** [16]**With unclean ones, mockers at feasts, gnashing at me with their teeth.** [17]𐤉𐤄𐤅𐤄, *how long would You look on? Rescue my being from their destructions, my only life from the lions.* [18]*I give You thanks in the great assembly; I praise You among a mighty people.* [19]*Let not my lying enemies rejoice over me; or those who hate me without cause wink their eyes.* [20]*For they do not speak peace, but they devise words of deceit against the peaceable ones of the land.* [21]*And they open their mouth wide against me, they said,* **"Aha, Aha***! Our eyes have seen it."* [22]*This You have seen, O* 𐤉𐤄𐤅𐤄; *do not be silent. O* 𐤉𐤄𐤅𐤄, *do not be far from me.* [23]*Stir up Yourself and awake to my right-ruling – to my cause, my Elohim and my Master.* [24]*Rule me rightly, O* 𐤉𐤄𐤅𐤄 *my Elohim, according to Your righteousness; and let them not rejoice over me.* [25]*Let them not say in their hearts,* **"Aha, our desire!" Let them not say, "We have swallowed him up."**

Tears in a Bottle

I am not afraid of the ten thousands of people against Me!

Psalms 3

O ayaz, *how my adversaries have increased! Many rising up against me.* [2]*Many are saying of me, "There is no deliverance for him in Elohim." Selah.* [3]*But You, O ayaz, are a shield for me, my esteem, and the One lifting up my head.* [4]*I cried to ayaz with my voice, and He heard me from His set-apart mountain. Selah.* [5]*I, I laid down and slept; I awoke, for ayaz sustained me.* [6]**I am not afraid of ten thousands of people who have set themselves against me all around.** [7]*Arise, O ayaz; Save me, O my Elohim! Because You have smitten all my enemies on the cheek; You have broken the teeth of the wrong.* [8]*Deliverance belongs to ayaz. Your blessing is on Your people. Selah.*

I am weary with my groaning!

Psalms 6

O ayaz, *rebuke me not in thine anger, neither chasten me in thy hot displeasure. Have mercy upon me, O ayaz; for I am weak: O ayaz, heal me; for my bones are vexed. My soul is also sore vexed: but thou, O ayaz, how long? Return, O ayaz, deliver my soul: oh save me for thy mercies' sake. For in death there is no remembrance of thee: in the grave who shall give thee thanks? I am weary with my groaning; all the night make I my bed to swim; I water my couch with my tears. Mine eye is consumed because of grief; it waxeth old because of all mine enemies. Depart from me, all ye workers of iniquity; for ayaz hath heard the voice of my weeping. ayaz hath heard my supplication; ayaz will receive my prayer. Let all mine enemies be ashamed and sore vexed: let them return and be ashamed suddenly.*

My mouth would not transgress!

Psalms 17

Hear righteousness, ayaz, Listen to my cry; Give ear to my prayer, from lips without deceit. [2]*Let my right-ruling go out from Your presence; let Your eyes see what is straight.* [3]**You have examined my heart; You have visited me in the night; You have tried me – You find I have not schemed; my mouth would not transgress.** [4]**As for the deeds of men – by the word of Your lips, I have kept myself from the paths of the destroyer.**

Tears in a Bottle

I am satisfied to see Your appearance, when I awake!
Psalms 17, cont.

[5]*My steps have held fast to Your paths, my feet have not slipped.* [6]*I have called upon You, for You answer me, O El; incline Your ear to me, hear my speech.* [7]*Let Your kindness be distinguished, You who save by Your right hand those who take refuge from those who rise up.* [8]*Guard me as the apple* **(pupil)** *of Your eye. Hide me under the shadow of Your wings,* [9]*from the face of the wrong who ravage me, from my deadly enemies who surround me.* [10]*They are enclosed in their own fat, they speak proudly with their mouths,* [11]*They have now surrounded us in our steps, they set their eyes to cast us to the ground,* [12]*Like a lion who is eager to tear his prey, and as a young lion crouching in cover.* [13]*Arise, O ⋎Y⋏Ƶ, confront him, cause him to bend; deliver my being from the wrong by Your sword,* [14]*From men by Your hand, O ⋎Y⋏Ƶ, from men of the world whose portion is in this life, and You fill their bellies with Your treasure, they are satisfied with children, and shall leave their riches to their babes.* [15]***As for me, let Me see Your face in righteousness; I am satisfied to see Your appearance when I awake.***

He has worn out my flesh and my skin!
Ekah (Lamentations) 3

I am the man who has seen affliction by the rod of His wrath. [2]*He has led me and made me walk in darkness and not light.* [3]*Indeed, He has turned back, He has turned His hand against me all the day.* [4]***He has worn out my flesh and my skin, He has broken (destroyed) my bones.*** [5]*He has piled up against me, and surrounded me with bitterness and hardship.* [6]***He has made me dwell in dark places like the dead of old.*** [7]*He has hedged me in and I do not go out, He has made my chain heavy.* [8]*Also, when I cry and shout, He shuts out my prayer.* [9]*He has blocked my ways with hewn stone, He has made my paths crooked.* [10]*He is to me like a bear lying in wait, a lion in hiding.* [11]*He has turned aside my ways and torn me in pieces, He has laid me waste.* [12]*He has bent His bow and set me up as a target for the arrow.* [13]*He made the arrows of His quiver pierce my kidneys.* [14]***I have been a mockery to all my people, their mocking song all the day.*** [15]*He has filled me with bitterness, He drenched me with wormwood.* [16]*And He has broken my teeth with gravel, He has covered me with ashes.* [17]*And You have removed my being far from peace, I have forgotten goodness.* [18]*And I said, "My strength and my expectancy have perished from ⋎Y⋏Ƶ."*

For though He afflicted, yet He shall show compassion!

Ekah (Lamentations) 3

[19]Remember my affliction and my anguish, the wormwood and the **gall.** [20]Your being indeed remembers and bows down upon me. [21]This I recall to my mind, therefore I wait: [22]The kindnesses of יהוה! **For we have not been consumed, for His compassions have not ended.** [23]**They are new every morning, great is Your trustworthiness.** [24]"יהוה is my portion," says my being, **"Therefore I wait for Him!"** [25] יהוה is good to those waiting for Him, to the being who seeks Him. [26]**It is good – both to wait and to be silent, for the deliverance of יהוה.** [27]It is good for a man to bear a yoke in his youth. [28]Let him sit alone and be silent, because He has laid it on him. [29]Let him put his mouth in the dust, there might yet be expectancy. [30]Let him give his cheek to the one who smites him – He is filled with reproach. [31]**For יהוה does not cast off forever.** [32]**For though He afflicted, yet He shall show compassion according to the greatness of His kindnesses.** [33]For He has not afflicted from His heart, nor does He grieve the children of men. [34]To crush under His feet all the prisoners of the earth, [35]To turn aside the right-ruling of man before the face of the Most High, [36]Or wrong a man in his cause – This יהוה does not approve. [37]Who was it that spoke, and it came to be! Has יהוה not commanded it? [38]Do not the evils and the good come out of the mouth of the Most High? [39]What? Should mankind complain, a living man, because of his sins? [40]Let us search and examine our ways, and turn back to יהוה. [41]Let us lift our hearts and hands to El in the heavens and say: [42]We, we have transgressed and rebelled. You, you have not forgiven. [43]You have wrapped Yourself with displeasure and pursued us. You have slain, You have not shown compassion. [44]You have wrapped Yourself with a cloud, so that prayer does not pass through. [45]You make us as scum and refuse in the midst of the peoples. [46]All our enemies have opened their mouth against us. [47]Fear and a snare have come upon us, shame and ruin. [48]Streams of water run down my eye for the ruin of the daughter of my people. [49]My eye flows out and does not cease, without stopping, [50]until יהוה looks down and sees from the heavens. [51]My eye pains my being because of all the daughters of my city. [52]My enemies hunted me down like a bird, without cause. [53]They have cut off my life in the pit, and they threw stones at me. [54]Waters flowed over my head; I said, "I am cut off!" [55]I called on Your Name, O יהוה, from the lowest pit.

Tears in a Bottle

My wounds have become stinky!

Psalms 38

O ⱯⲨⱯⵣ, do not rebuke me in Your wrath, nor chastise me in Your hot displeasure! [2]For Your arrows have pierced me, and Your hand comes down on me. [3]There is no soundness in my flesh because of Your rage, nor peace in my bones because of my sin. (the sins of others) [4]For my crookednesses have passed over my head; like a heavy burden, too heavy for me. [5]My wounds have become stinky, festering because of my folly. [6]I have been bent down; I have been bowed down very much; all day long I have gone mourning. [7]For my loins have become filled with burning, and there is no soundness in my flesh. [8]I have become weak and greatly crushed; I howled from the groaning of my heart. [9]ⱯⲨⱯⵣ, all my desire is before You; and my sighing has not been hid from You. [10]My heart is throbbing, my strength has forsaken me; And the light of my eyes also is not with me. [11]My loved ones and my friends stand back from my plague, and my neighbors stand far away. [12]And those seeking my life lay a snare; and those seeking my evil have spoken of destruction, and utter deceit all day long. [13]But I, as one deaf, do not hear; and as a dumb one who does not open his mouth. [14]I am like a man who does not hear, and who has no rebukes in his mouth. [15]For on You, O ⱯⲨⱯⵣ, I have waited; You do answer, O ⱯⲨⱯⵣ my Elohim. [16]For I said, "Otherwise they would rejoice over me, when my foot slips they would exalt themselves over me." [17]For I am ready to fall, and my pain is always with me. [18]For I confess my crookedness; I am sorry over my sin (The sins of others that Yahushua carried!).

[19]But my enemies are alive; they have become strong; and those hating me falsely are many. [20]And those who repay evil for good, they oppose me, because I follow what is good. [21]Do not forsake me, O ⱯⲨⱯⵣ; O my Elohim, be not far from me! [22]Hasten to help me, O ⱯⲨⱯⵣ, my deliverance!

Tears in a Bottle

Evils without number have surrounded Me!

Psalms 40

And He inclined to me, and heard my cry. [2]And He drew me out of the pit of destruction, out of the muddy clay, and He set my feet upon a rock, He is establishing my steps. [3]Then He put a new song in my mouth; praise to our Elohim; many do see it and fear, and trust in 𐤉𐤄𐤅𐤄. *[4]Blessed is that man who has made* 𐤉𐤄𐤅𐤄 *his trust, and has not turned to the proud, and those turning aside to falsehood. [5]O* 𐤉𐤄𐤅𐤄 *my Elohim, many are the wonders which You have done, and Your purposes toward us; there is no one to compare with You; I declare and speak: they are too many to be numbered. [6]Slaughtering [2]and meal offering You did not desire; You have opened my ears; burnt offering and sin offering You did not ask for. [7]Then I said, "See, I have come; in the scroll of the Book it is prescribed for me. [8]I have delighted to do Your pleasure, O my Elohim, and Your Torah is within my heart." [9]__I have proclaimed the good news of righteousness,__ in the great assembly; see, I do not restrain my lips, O* 𐤉𐤄𐤅𐤄, *You know. [10]I did not conceal Your righteousness within my heart; I have declared Your trustworthiness and Your deliverance; I did not hide Your kindness and Your truth From the great assembly. [11]Do not withhold Your compassion from me, O* 𐤉𐤄𐤅𐤄; *let Your kindness and Your truth always watch over me. [12]__For evils without number__ have surrounded me; my crookednesses have overtaken me, and I have been unable to see; they became more than the hairs of my head; and my heart has failed me. [13]Be pleased, O* 𐤉𐤄𐤅𐤄, *to deliver me; O* 𐤉𐤄𐤅𐤄, *hasten to help me! [14]Let those who seek to destroy my life be ashamed and abashed altogether; let those who are desiring my evil be driven back and put to shame. [15]Let those who say to me, "__Aha, Aha__"! Be appalled at their own shame. [16]Let all those who seek You rejoice and be glad in You; let those who love Your deliverance always say, "*𐤉𐤄𐤅𐤄 *be exalted!"*

Psalms 41

Blessed is he who considers the poor; 𐤉𐤄𐤅𐤄 *does deliver him in a day of evil. [2]* 𐤉𐤄𐤅𐤄 *does guard him and keep him alive; he is blessed on the earth, and You do not hand him over to the desire of his enemies. [3]* 𐤉𐤄𐤅𐤄 *sustains him on his sickbed; in his weakness on his bed You bring a change.*

Tears in a Bottle

Psalms 41, cont.
⁴As for me, I said, "O 𐤀𐤉𐤀𐤆, show me favor; heal me, for I have sinned (the sins of others) against You." ⁵My enemies speak evil of me, "When he dies his name shall perish." ⁶And when one comes to visit, he speaks falsely; his heart gathers wickedness to itself; he goes out, he speaks of it. ⁷All who hate me whisper together against me; they plot evil to me, saying, ⁸"A matter of Beliya'al is poured out on him, that when he lies down, he would not rise again." ⁹Even my own friend in whom I trusted, who ate my bread, has lifted up his heel against me. ¹⁰But You, 𐤀𐤉𐤀𐤆, show me favor and raise me up, and let me repay them. ¹¹By this I know that You did delight in me, because my enemy does not shout for joy over me.

My tears have been my food day and night!

Psalms 42
As a deer longs for the water streams, so my being longs for You, O Elohim. ²My being thirsts for Elohim, for the living El. When shall I enter in to appear before Elohim? ³My tears have been my food day and night, while they say to me all day, "Where is your Elohim?" ⁴These I remember, and pour out my being within me. For I used to pass along with the throng; I went with them to the House of Elohim, with the voice of joy and praise, a multitude keeping a festival! ⁵Why are you depressed, O my being? And why are you restless within me? Wait for Elohim: for I shall yet thank Him, for the deliverance of His face! ⁶O my Elohim, my being is depressed within me; therefore I remember You from the land of the Yarden, and from the heights of Hermon, from Mount Mits'ar. ⁷Deep calls to deep at the sound of Your waterfalls; all Your waves and breakers passed over me. ⁸By day 𐤀𐤉𐤀𐤆 commands His kindness, and by night His song is with me; a prayer to the El of my life. ⁹I say to El my Rock, "Why have You forgotten me? Why do I go mourning because of the oppression of the enemy?" ¹⁰My enemies have reproached me, like a crushing of my bones, while they say to me all day long, "Where is your Elohim?"

Tears in a Bottle

They hate Me!

Psalms 55

Give ear to my prayer, O Elohim, and do not hide Yourself from my plea. ^{2}*Give heed to me, and answer me;* **I wander and moan in my complaint,** ^{3}**because of the noise of the enemy, because of the outcry of the wrong; for they bring down wickedness upon me, And in wrath <u>they hate me</u>.** ^{4}**My heart is pained within me, and the frights of death have fallen upon me.** ^{5}**<u>Fear and trembling</u> have come upon me, and <u>shuddering covers me</u>.**

It was you, a man My equal, My companion and My Friend!

^{6}*And I said, "Who would give me wings like a dove! I would fly away and be at rest.* ^{7}*"See, I would wander far off, I would lodge in the wilderness. Selah.* ^{8}*"I would hasten my escape from the raging wind and storm."* ^{9}**Confuse, O ayaz, divide their tongues, for I saw violence and strife in the city.** ^{10}**Day and night they go around it on its walls; wickedness and trouble are also in the midst of it.** ^{11}**Covetings are in its midst; oppression and deceit do not vanish from its streets.** ^{12}**It is not an enemy who reproaches me – that I could bear; nor one who hates me who is making himself great against me – Then I could hide from him.** ^{13}**But it was <u>you, a man my equal, my companion and my friend</u>.** ^{14}**We took sweet counsel together, we walked to the House of Elohim in the throng.** ^{15}*Let death come upon them; let them go down into the grave alive, for evil is in their dwellings, in their midst.* ^{16}*I, I call upon Elohim, and ayaz saves me.* ^{17}**Evening and morning and at noon I complain and <u>moan</u>, and He hears my voice.** ^{18}**He has redeemed my life in peace from the battle against me, for there were many against me.** ^{19}*El, even He who sits enthroned from of old, does hear and afflict them – Selah – Those with whom there are no changes, those who do not fear Elohim.* ^{20}*He has put forth his hands against those, who were at peace with him; He has broken his covenant.* ^{21}*His mouth was smoother than curds, yet in his heart is fighting; His words were softer than oil, but they are drawn swords.* ^{22}**Cast your burden on ayaz, and let Him sustain you; <u>He never allows the righteous to be shaken</u>.** ^{23}*For You, O Elohim, do bring them down to the pit of destruction; men of blood and deceit do not reach half their days; but I,* **<u>I trust in You</u>.**

Tears in a Bottle

You put My tears into Your Bottle!

Psalms 56

Show me favor, O Elohim, for man would swallow me up; fighting all day long, he oppresses me. **[2]My enemies would swallow me up all day long, for many are fighting against me, O Most High.** [3]*In the day I am afraid, I trust in You.* [4]*In Elohim, whose word I praise, in Elohim I have trusted; I do not fear; what could flesh do to me?* **[5]All day long they twist my words; all their thoughts are against me for evil.** **[6]They stir up strife, they hide, they watch my steps, as they lie in wait for my life.** **[7]Because of wickedness, cast them out. Put down the peoples in displeasure, O Elohim!** **[8]You have counted my wanderings; YOU PUT MY TEARS INTO YOUR BOTTLE; are they not in Your book?** [9]*My enemies turn back in the day I call;* <u>**this I know, because Elohim is for me.**</u> [10]*In Elohim, whose Word I praise, In* ᴀYᴀz*, whose Word I praise,* **[11]In Elohim I have trusted; I do not fear; what could man do to me?** [12]*On me, O Elohim, are Your vows; I render praises to You,* [13]*For You have delivered my life from death, my feet from stumbling, that I might walk before Elohim, in the light of the living!*

Shame has covered my face!

Psalms 69

[3]<u>*I am worn out from my crying;*</u> *my throat is dry; my eyes grow dim as I wait for my Elohim.* [4]*Those* <u>who hate me without a cause are more than the hairs of my head</u>*; they are mighty who would destroy me, my lying enemies;* <u>what I did not steal, I restored</u>. [5]*O Elohim, You Yourself know my foolishness; and my guilt has not been hidden from You.* [6]*Let not those who wait for You, O Master* ᴀYᴀz *of hosts, Be ashamed because of me; let not those who seek You Be humbled because of me, O Elohim of Yisra'el.* [7]<u>*Because I have borne reproach for Your sake; shame has covered my face.*</u> [8]<u>*I have become a stranger to my brothers, and a foreigner to my mother's children;*</u> [9]<u>*because ardor for Your house has eaten me up, and the reproaches of those who reproach You have fallen on me*</u>. [10]*And I wept in my being with fasting, and it became my reproach.* [11]*And when* <u>I put on sackcloth</u>, <u>I became a proverb to them.</u>

Tears in a Bottle

I am the song of drunkards!

Psalms 69, cont.

¹²**They who sit in the gate talk about me, and I am the song of the drunkards.** ¹³*But as for me, my prayer is to You, O 𐤉𐤄𐤅𐤄, at an acceptable time, O Elohim. In the greatness of Your kindness, answer me in the truth of Your deliverance.* ¹⁴*Rescue me out of the mire, and let me not sink. Let me be rescued from those who hate me, and out of the deep waters.* ¹⁵*Let not a flood of waters overflow me, nor let the deep swallow me up, nor let the pit shut its mouth on me.* ¹⁶*Answer me, O 𐤉𐤄𐤅𐤄, for Your kindness is good. According to the greatness of Your compassion, turn to me.* ¹⁷**And do not hide Your face from Your servant, for I am in distress; answer me speedily.**

Reproach has broken My Heart and I am Sick!

¹⁹*You Yourself know my reproach, and my shame and my confusion; my adversaries are all before You.* ²⁰<u>**Reproach has broken my heart and I am sick; I looked for sympathy, but there was none; and for comforters, but I found none.**</u> ²¹*And they gave me gall for my food, and for my thirst* <u>*they gave me vinegar to drink.*</u> ²²*Let their table before them become a snare, and a trap to those at ease.* ²³**Let their eyes be darkened, so as not to see; and make their loins shake continually.** ²⁴*Pour out Your wrath upon them, and let Your burning displeasure overtake them.* ²⁵**Let their encampments be deserted; let no one dwell in their tents.** ²⁶*For they persecute him* **whom You have smitten, and talk about the pain of those You have wounded.** ²⁷*Add crookedness to their crookedness, and let them not enter into Your righteousness.* ²⁸*Let them be blotted out of the book of the living, and not be written with the righteous.* ²⁹*But* <u>**I am poor and in pain**</u>*; let Your deliverance, O Elohim, set me up on high.* ³⁰*I praise the name of Elohim with a song, and I make Him great with thanksgiving.* ³¹*And this pleases* 𐤉𐤄𐤅𐤄 *more than an ox, a bull with horns and hooves.* ³²*The humble shall see, they rejoice, You who seek Elohim, and your hearts live.* ³³*For* 𐤉𐤄𐤅𐤄 *hears the poor, and He shall not despise His captives.*

Psalms 70

O Elohim, deliver me! Hasten to my help, O 𐤉𐤄𐤅𐤄*!* ²**Let those who seek my life be ashamed and abashed, let those who are desiring my evil be turned back and humiliated.** ³**Let those who say, "<u>Aha, Aha</u>!" be turned back because of their shame.**

Tears in a Bottle

You are my help and my deliverer!

Psalms 70, cont.
⁴Let all those who seek You rejoice and be glad in You; and let those, who love Your deliverance always say, "Let Elohim be made great!" *⁵But I am poor and needy; hasten to me, O Elohim! You are my help and my deliverer;* O ᴬYᴬZ, *do not delay.*

Psalms 140
Rescue me, O ᴬYᴬZ, *from men of evil; preserve me from men of violence, ²who have devised evils in their hearts;* __they stir up conflicts all day long__. *³They sharpen their tongues like a snake; the poison of cobras is under their lips. Selah. ⁴Guard me, O* ᴬYᴬZ, *from the hands of the wrong; guard me from a man of violence, who have* __schemed to trip up my steps__. *⁵The proud have hidden a trap for me, and cords; they have spread a net by the wayside; they have set snares for me. Selah. ⁶I said to* ᴬYᴬZ, *"You are my El; Hear the voice of my prayers, O* ᴬYᴬZ. *⁷"O Master* ᴬYᴬZ, *my saving strength, You have screened my head in the day of battle. ⁸"Do not grant the desires of the wrong, O* ᴬYᴬZ; *do not promote his scheme. Selah. ⁹"Those who surround me lift up their head; the trouble of their lips cover them; ¹⁰"* **Let burning coals fall on them; let them be made to fall into the fire, Into deep pits, let them not rise again.** *¹¹"Let not a slanderer be established in the earth; let evil hunt the man of violence speedily." ¹²I have known that* ᴬYᴬZ *maintains the cause of the afflicted, the right-ruling of the poor. ¹³Only, let the righteous give thanks to Your name, let the straight ones dwell in Your presence.*

No refuge remains to Me; no one inquires after My being!

Psalms 142
I cry out to ᴬYᴬZ *with my voice; I pray to* ᴬYᴬZ *with my voice. ²I pour out my complaint before Him; I declare before Him my distress. ³When my spirit grew faint within me,* **then You know my path.** *In the way in which I walk they have hidden a trap for me. ⁴Look to the right hand and see, and* __no one is concerned for me__; __no refuge remains to me; no one inquires after my being__. *⁵I cried out to You, O* ᴬYᴬZ: *I said, "You are my refuge, my portion in the land of the living. ⁶"Listen to* __my cry__, __For I am brought very low__; *deliver me from my persecutors, for they are too strong for me.*

Tears in a Bottle

My heart within Me is stunned!

Psalms 143

Hear my prayer, O **ⱯYⱯZ**, *give ear to my pleadings in Your trustworthiness. Answer me in Your righteousness. [2]And do not enter into right-ruling with Your servant, for before You no one living is in the right. [3]For the <u>enemy has pursued my being</u>; he has crushed my life to the ground; <u>he has made me dwell in dark places</u>, like the dead of old. [4]Therefore my spirit grew faint within me, my heart within me is stunned. [5]<u>I remembered the days of old</u>; I <u>meditated on all Your works</u>; I ponder on the work of Your hands. [6]I have spread out my hands to You; my being is like a thirsty land for You. Selah. [7]Hasten, answer me, O* **ⱯYⱯZ**; *my spirit fails! Do not hide Your face from me, lest I be like those going down into the pit. [8]Let me hear Your kindness in the morning, for in You I have put my trust; let me know the way in which I should walk, for I have lifted up my being to You. [9]Deliver me from my enemies, O* **ⱯYⱯZ**; *I take refuge in You. [10]Teach me to do Your good pleasure, for You are my Elohim. Let Your good Spirit lead me In the land of straightness. [11]For the sake of Your name, O* **ⱯYⱯZ**, *revive me! In Your righteousness, bring my being out of distress. [12]And in Your kindness, cut off my enemies, and destroy all the adversaries of my life, for I am Your servant!*

I have become a taunt song for the rebellious!

Dead Sea Scrolls
Thanksgiving Scroll

Col 10 (1QH = 4Q432 Frag 3)

*So I became a <u>trap for the rebellious</u>, and <u>a cure for all who turn from rebellion</u>; prudence for the fool, and a steadfast mind for the reckless. You have appointed me as <u>an object of shame and derision</u> to the faithless, but a foundation of truth and understanding for the upright. And because of the iniquity of the wicked, I have become slander on the lips of the brutal, and **scoffers gnash their teeth**. I have become a <u>taunt song for the rebellious</u>, and the assembly of the wicked have stormed against me. They roar like a gale on the seas, when their waves churn, they cast up slime and mud. But you have appointed me as a banner for the chosen of righteousness, and an informed mediator of the wonderful mysteries, so as to test [the men] of truth and to try the lovers of correction.*

Tears in a Bottle

Thanksgiving Scroll, Col 10, cont.

I have become impassioned against those who seek flat[tery], [so that all] the men of deceit roar against me, as the sound of the thunder of mighty waters. [All] their thoughts are as the plots of Belial (Satan the liar) and they have transformed a man's life, whom You established by my word and whom You taught understanding, into pitfall. You placed it in His heart to open up the source of knowledge to all who understand. But they have changed them, through uncircumcised lips and a straight message, into a people with no understanding, that they might be ruined in their delusion.

Thanksgiving Scroll
All My friends and acquaintances have been driven away!

Col 10, cont.

*You have revealed yourself to me. But these Your people [go astray]. Fo[r] they flatter themselves with words, and mediators of deceit lead them astray, so that they are ruined without knowledge. For [...] their works are deceitful, for good works were rejected by them. **Neither did they esteem me; even when You displayed Your might through me. Instead they drove me out from the land as a bird from its nest. And all my friends and acquaintances have been driven away from me; they esteem me as a ruined vessel.** But they are mediators of a lie and seers of deceit. They have plotted wickedness against me, so as to exchange Your law, which You spoke distinctly in my heart, for flattering words directed to your people. They hold back the drink of knowledge from those that thirst, and for their thirst they give them vinegar to drink, that they might observe their error behaving madly at their festivals and getting caught in their nets.*

Col 13

You assigned my dwelling with many fishermen**, they who spread their net on the surface of the water and hunt for the children of injustice. **You have established me there for judgment**. You have strengthened the counsel of truth in my heart, and waters of the covenant for those that seek it. But You shut the mouth of the young lions whose teeth are like a sword, and whose fangs are as a sharp spear. **All their evil plans for abduction are like poison of serpents; they lie in wait, but have not opened their mouths wide against me.

Tears in a Bottle

Thanksgiving Scroll

Grief and misery surround Me, and shame is upon My face!

Col 13

For you my Elohim, have concealed me from the children of men, and your law You have hidden in [me] until the time You reveal Your salvation to me. For in my soul's distress You did not abandon me, but You heard my cry in the bitterness of my soul. You recognized my grievous cry by my sigh and You delivered the life of the destitute one from the den of lions, who sharpen their tongue as a sword. And You, O my Elohim, have shut their teeth, lest they tear the soul of the destitute and poor to pieces. And their tongue is drawn in as a sword into its sheath, so that it might not strike the soul of your servant. And so that you might make me great against the children of men, You have done wondrous deeds with the poor. **You have brought him into the <u>crucib[le like g]old to be worked by the fire, and as silver, which is refined in the smelter of the smiths to be refined seven times</u>. But the wicked of the people rush against me with their afflictions, and all the day long they crush my soul….But I myself have become […], <u>strife</u>, <u>and contention for my fellows</u>, <u>jealously</u>, <u>and anger to those</u>, <u>who have entered my covenant</u>, <u>a grumbling and a complaining to all</u>, <u>who are my comrades</u>. Ev[en] those who sha[re] my bread have lifted up their heal against me, and all those who have committed themselves to my counsel speak perversely against me with unjust lips. <u>The men of my [coun]cil rebel and grumble round about</u>. <u>And concerning the mystery which you hid in me</u>, they go about as slanderers to the children of destruction.** Because [You] have exal[ted Yourself] in me, and for sake of their guilt, You have hidden in me the spring of understanding and the counsel of truth. But they devise the ruination of their heart; [and with words of] Belial they have exhibited a lying tongue; as the poison of serpents it bursts forth continuously. As those who crawl in the dust, they cast forth to sei[ze the cunning smiles] to tumble and putting an end to my strength so that I might not stand firm. **They overtake me in narrow places, where there is no place of refuge, nor when they […]. <u>They intone their dispute against me on the lyre</u>, <u>and compose their complaint to music</u>; together with ruin and desolation. <u>Searing pains have se[ized me] and pangs as the convulsions of one giving birth</u>.**

Tears in a Bottle

Thanksgiving Scroll

Grief and misery surround Me, and shame is upon My face!

Col 13, cont.

*My heart is tormented within me. I have put on the garment of mourning and **my tongue clings to the roof of my mouth**. For they have surrounded me [with...] of their heart, and their desire has appeared to me as bitterness. The light of my countenance becomes dark, and my splendor is transformed to gloom.* But You , O my Elohim, have opened a wide space in my heart, **but they continue to press in, and they shut me up in deep darkness**, so that I eat the bread of groaning , and my drink is tears without end. For **my eyes have become weak** from anger and my soul by daily bitterness. *Grief and misery surround me, and shame is upon my face*. My bread has become strife, and my drink contention. They enter my bones, causing my spirit to stumble and putting an end to my strength.

Dead Sea Scrolls
Thanksgiving Scroll

All this is because of the ruin caused by their Sin!

Col 15

*[...] I am speechless [...] these [...] [...] **my [a]rm is shattered at the shoulder**, and my foot has sunk in the mire. My eyes are sealed shut from seeing evil, my ears from hearing of bloodshed, and **my heart is stupefied because of evil plotting**. For Belial is manifest when the true nature of their being is revealed. All the foundations of my frame crumble. **My bones are separated**, and **my bowels are like a ship in a raging storm**. My heart roars as to destruction, and **a spirit of staggering overwhelms me**. All BECAUSE OF THE RUIN CAUSED BY THEIR SIN!*

Col 16

*[My] **dwelling is with the sick**, and [my] heart k[no]ws **agonies**. I have become like a man who is forsaken by an **incurable pain without stopping**. [...ro]ars over me like those, who descend into Sheol. Among the dead my spirit searches for my li[fe] goes down to the pit [...] **my soul is faint day and night without rest**.*

Tears in a Bottle

Dead Sea Scrolls
Thanksgiving Scroll

Col 16, cont.

And my agony breaks out as a <u>burning fire shut up within [my] b[ones]</u> whose flame consumes for days on end, putting an end to my strength without ceasing and <u>destroying my flesh without end</u>. The billows break over me and my heart is poured out as water, and my flesh is melted as wax. The strength of my loins has become a calamity, <u>my arm is broken from the shoulder</u>, [and <u>I am no]t [able] to swing my hand</u>. My [foo]t is caught in fetters, my knees become as water, and <u>I am not able to take a step</u>; <u>there is no sound to the tread of my feet</u>. [...] are pulled loose by stumbling chains, and <u>my tongue You had exalted in my mouth, but no longer</u>. <u>No more can my [tong]ue give forth its voice for instru[ction] to revive the spirits of those who stumble, and to support the weary with a word</u>.

Col 17

*My bed lifts up a lamentation, [and my pallet] a <u>**sound of groanings**</u>, my eyes are as a moth in a furnace, and <u>**my weeping is as brooks of water**</u>. <u>**My eyes fail for rest**</u>, [and...] stands at great distance from me, and <u>**my life has been set aside**</u>.*

Dead Sea Scrolls
Thanksgiving Scroll

I shall choose My judgment, and with My agony I am satisfied!

Col 17, cont.

But as for me, <u>from ruin to desolation</u>, <u>from pain to agony</u>, and <u>from travails to torments</u> <u>my soul meditates on your wonders</u>. In your mercy You have <u>not</u> rejected me. Time and time again my soul delights in the abundance of your compassion. I give an answer to those who would wipe me out, and reproof to those who would cast me down. I will condemn his verdict, but Your judgment I honor, for I know Your truth. <u>I shall choose my judgment</u>, and with my agony I am satisfied for I have waited upon Your mercy. You have put a supplication in the mouth of Your servant, and You have not rebuked my life, nor have You removed my well-being. You have not forsaken my hope, but in the face of affliction, You have restored my spirit. For You have established my spirit and know my deliberations.

Dead Sea Scrolls
Thanksgiving Scroll

Col 17, cont.

In my distress <u>You have soothed me</u>, <u>and I delight in forgiveness</u>. But You, O my ᗋYᗋZ, for [...] You plead my case. For in the mystery of Your wisdom, You have reproved me. You hide the truth in [its time until...] its appointed time. **Your chastisement has become joy and gladness to me and my agonies have become an et[ernal] healing and unending [...]. The contempt of my enemies have become a glorious crown for me, and my stumbling, eternal strength.**

Col 22

But my <u>heart groans</u> [...] and my heart melts as wax because of the transgressions and sin. [...] Blessed are you, O ᗋYᗋZ of knowledge, because You have determined [...] and <u>this happened to Your servant for Your sake.</u>

Every single time, when I read those passages, My heart is pricked to the core! After you have meditated on those passages yourself, I believe that you will have a new appreciation of the love that Yahushua has in His heart for you! Tragically, most people in this world don't really care at all about OWYᗋZ! **They don't care about Yahushua's feelings** or His sufferings! May ᗋYᗋZ reach out to them in His mercy and lift the veil that covers their blinded eyes so that they will see!

Bless ᗋYᗋZ!
Bless ᗋYᗋZ!
Bless ᗋYᗋZ!
Bless ᗋYᗋZ!
Bless ᗋYᗋZ!

Songs of the Suffering Servant

Song #1
YeshaYahu (Isaiah) 42
*Behold my servant, whom I uphold; mine elect, in whom my soul delighteth; **I have put my spirit upon him**: He shall bring forth judgment to the Gentiles. He shall not cry, nor lift up, nor cause his voice to be heard in the street. A bruised reed shall He not break, and the smoking flax shall He not quench: He shall bring forth judgment unto truth. He shall not fail nor be discouraged, till He have set judgment in the earth: and the isles shall wait for his law. Thus saith El Ɐ𐤟Ɀ, He that created the heavens, and stretched them out; He that spread forth the earth, and that which cometh out of it; He that giveth breath unto the people upon it, and spirit to them that walk therein: **I Ɐ𐤟Ɀ have called thee in righteousness, and will hold thine hand, and will keep thee, and give thee for a covenant of the people, for a light of the Gentiles; to open the blind eyes, to bring out the prisoners from the prison, and them that sit in darkness out of the prison house.***

Song #2
YeshaYahu (Isaiah) 49
Listen, O isles, unto me; and hearken, ye people, from far; Ɐ𐤟Ɀ hath **called Me from the womb; <u>from the bowels of my mother hath he made mention of my name</u>. And he hath made my mouth like a sharp sword**; *in the shadow of his hand hath he hid me, and made me a polished shaft; in his quiver hath he hid me; and said unto me, Thou art my servant, O Israel, in whom I will be glorified. Then I said, I have labored in vain, I have spent my strength for naught, and in vain: yet surely my judgment is with Ɐ𐤟Ɀ, and my work with my Elohim.* **And now, saith Ɐ𐤟Ɀ that formed me from the womb to be his servant, to bring Jacob again to him,** *Though Israel be not gathered, yet shall I be glorious in the eyes of Ɐ𐤟Ɀ, and my Elohim shall be my strength.* **And he said, <u>it is a light thing that thou shouldest be my servant to raise up the tribes of Jacob,</u> and to restore the preserved of Israel: I will also give thee for a light to the Gentiles, that thou mayest be <u>my salvation unto the end of the earth</u>.**

Tears in a Bottle

Song #2

YeshaYahu (Isaiah) 49, cont.

Thus saith ⟨AYAZ⟩, the Redeemer of Israel, and his Holy One, to him whom man despiseth, to him whom the nation abhorreth, to a servant of rulers, Kings shall see and arise, princes also shall worship, because of ⟨AYAZ⟩ that is faithful, and he Holy One of Israel, and He shall choose thee. Thus saith ⟨AYAZ⟩, in an acceptable time have I heard thee, and in a day of salvation have I helped thee: and I will preserve thee, and give thee for a covenant of the people, to establish the earth, to cause to inherit the desolate heritages; that thou mayest say to the prisoners, go forth; to them that are in darkness, shew yourselves. They shall feed in the ways, and their pastures shall be in all high places. They shall not hunger nor thirst; neither shall the heat nor sun smite them: for he that hath mercy on them shall lead them, even by the springs of water shall he guide them. And I will make all my mountains a way, and my highways shall be exalted. Behold, these shall come from far: and, lo, these from the north and from the west; and these from the land of Sinim. Sing, O heavens; and be joyful, O earth; and break forth into singing, O mountains: for ⟨AYAZ⟩ hath comforted his people, and will have mercy upon his afflicted. But Zion said, ⟨AYAZ⟩ hath forsaken me, and my master hath forgotten me. Can a woman forget her sucking child, that she should not have compassion on the son of her womb? Yea, they may forget, yet will I not forget thee. Behold, I have graven thee upon the palms of my hands; thy walls are continually before me. Thy children shall make haste; thy destroyers and they that made thee waste shall go forth of thee. Lift up thine eyes round about, and behold: all these gather themselves together, and come to thee. As I live, saith ⟨AYAZ⟩, thou shalt surely clothe thee with them all, as with an ornament, and bind them on thee, as a bride doeth. For thy waste and thy desolate places, and the land of thy destruction, shall even now be too narrow by reason of the inhabitants, and they that swallowed thee up shall be far away. The children which thou shalt have, after thou hast lost the other, shall say again in thine ears, The place is too strait for me: give place to me that I may dwell. Then shalt thou say in thine heart, Who hath begotten me these, seeing I have lost my children, and am desolate, a captive, and removing to and fro? and who hath brought up these? Behold, I was left alone; these, where had they been?

Tears in a Bottle

Song #2
YeshaYahu (Isaiah) 49, cont.
Thus saith the Master ⲀⲨⲀⳆ, behold, I will lift up mine hand to the Gentiles, and set up my standard to the people: and they shall bring thy sons in their arms, and thy daughters shall be carried upon their shoulders. And kings shall be thy nursing fathers, and their queens thy nursing mothers: they shall bow down to thee with their face toward the earth, and lick up the dust of thy feet; and thou shalt know that I am ⲀⲨⲀⳆ: for they shall not be ashamed that wait for me. Shall the prey be taken from the mighty, or the lawful captive delivered? But thus saith ⲀⲨⲀⳆ, even the captives of the mighty shall be taken away, and the prey of the terrible shall be delivered: for I will contend with him that contendeth with thee, and I will save thy children. And I will feed them that oppress thee with their own flesh; and they shall be drunken with their own blood, as with sweet wine: and all flesh shall know that I ⲀⲨⲀⳆ am thy Saviour and thy Redeemer, the mighty One of Jacob.

Song #3
YeshaYahu (Isaiah) 50
*The Master ⲀⲨⲀⳆ hath given Me the tongue of the learned, that I should know how to speak a word in season to him that is weary: He wakeneth morning by morning, He wakeneth mine ear to hear as the learned. The Master ⲀⲨⲀⳆ hath opened mine ear, and I was not rebellious, neither turned away back. I gave my back to the smiters, and my cheeks to them that plucked off the hair: **I hid not my face from shame and spitting.** For the Master ⲀⲨⲀⳆ will help Me; therefore shall I not be confounded: therefore have I set my face like a flint, and I know that I shall not be ashamed. He is near that justifieth Me; who will contend with Me? Let us stand together: who is mine adversary? let him come near to Me. Behold, the Master ⲀⲨⲀⳆ will help Me; who is he that shall condemn Me? Lo, they all shall wax old as a garment; the moth shall eat them up. Who is among you that feareth ⲀⲨⲀⳆ, that obeyeth the voice of his servant, that walketh in darkness, and hath no light? Let him trust in the name of ⲀⲨⲀⳆ, and stay upon his Elohim. Behold, all ye that kindle a fire, that compass yourselves about with sparks: walk in the light of your fire, and in the sparks that ye have kindled. This shall ye have of mine hand; ye shall lie down in sorrow.*

Song #4

YeshaYahu (Isaiah) 52

[14]As many were astonished at You – **so the disfigurement beyond any man's and His form beyond the sons of men** –[15]He shall likewise startle many nations. Sovereigns shut their mouths at Him, for what had not been recounted to them they shall see, and what they had not heard they shall understand.

YeshaYahu, (Isaiah) 53

<u>Who **has** believed **our report**</u>? And to whom was the arm of ayaz revealed? [2]For He grew up before Him as a tender plant, and as a root out of dry ground. *He has no form or splendor that we should look upon Him, nor appearance that we should desire Him –* [3]*despised and rejected by men, a <u>man of pains and knowing sickness</u>. And as one from whom the <u>face is hidden</u>, being despised, and we did not consider Him.* [4]*Truly, He has borne our sicknesses and carried our pains. Yet we reckoned Him stricken, smitten by Elohim, and afflicted.* [5]*But He was pierced for our transgressions, He was crushed for our crookednesses. The chastisement for our peace was upon Him, and by His stripes we are healed.* [6]*We all, like sheep, went astray, each one of us has turned to his own way. And ayaz has laid on Him the crookedness of us all.* [7]*He was oppressed and He was afflicted, but He did not open His mouth. He was led as a lamb to the slaughter, and as a sheep before its shearers is silent, but He did not open His mouth.* [8]*He was taken from prison and from judgment. And as for His generation, who considered that He shall be cut off from the land of the living? **For the transgression of My people He was stricken.*** [9]*And He was appointed a grave with the wrong, and with the rich at His death, because He had done no violence, nor was deceit in His mouth.* [10]*But ayaz was pleased to crush Him, <u>He laid sickness on Him</u>, that when He made Himself an offering for guilt, He would see a seed, He would prolong His days and the pleasure of ayaz prosper in His hand.* [11]*He would see the result of the suffering of His life and be satisfied. Through His knowledge My righteous servant makes many righteous, and He bears their crookednesses.* [12]*Therefore I give Him a portion among the great, and He divides the spoil with the strong, because He poured out His being unto death, and He was counted with the transgressors, and He bore the sin of many, and made intercession for the transgressors.*

Tears in a Bottle

The Babylonian Talmud of Orthodox Judaism documents a story about a Leper scholar! Could this be the anointed one of ⱿYⱿZ, our Rabbi? Could this be the "Teacher of Righteousness" written about by the writers of the Dead Sea Scrolls? You know the answer, don't you? Selah! Selah! Selah!

The Leper Scholar-Israel's Messiah

"The Messiah--what is his name? The Rabbis say, The Leper scholar, as it is said, `surely he has borne our griefs and carried our sorrows: yet we did esteem him a leper, smitten of Elohim and afflicted...'" (Sanhedrin 98b) The Talmud also "records" a supposed discourse between the great Rabbi Joshua Ben Levi and the prophet Elijah. The rabbi asks "When will the Messiah come?" And "By what sign may I recognize him?" Elijah tells the rabbi to go to the gate of the city where he will find the Messiah sitting among the poor lepers. The Messiah, says the prophet, sits bandaging his leprous sores one at a time, unlike the rest of the sufferers, who bandage them all at once. Why? Because He might be needed at any time and would not want to be delayed. Elijah says He will come "Today, if you will listen to his voice." (Sanhedrin 98a)

Remember this parable!
The Stone the Builders rejected has become the Cornerstone!

Luke 20

*Then began He to speak to the people this parable; a certain man planted a vineyard, and let it forth to husbandmen, and went into a far country for a long time. And at the season he sent a servant to the husbandmen, that they should give him of the fruit of the vineyard: but the husbandmen beat him, and sent him away empty. And again he sent another servant: and they beat him also, and entreated him shamefully, and sent him away empty. And again he sent a third: and they wounded him also, and cast him out. Then said the master of the vineyard, what shall I do? **I will send my beloved son**: it may be they will reverence him when they see him. **<u>But when the husbandmen saw him</u>, they reasoned among themselves, saying, this is the heir: come, let us kill him, that the inheritance may be ours**. So they cast him out of the vineyard, and killed him. What therefore shall the master of the vineyard do unto them? He shall come and destroy these husbandmen, and shall give the vineyard to others. And when they heard it, they said, let it not be.*

Tears in a Bottle

Luke 20, cont.
And he beheld them, and said, What is this then that is written, the **Stone** *which the builders rejected, the same is become the head of the corner?*

The Mystery of the Cornerstone and the end of the age
Daniel 2
Daniel answered in the presence of the king, and said, the secret which the king hath demanded cannot the wise men, the astrologers, the magicians, the soothsayers, shew unto the king; but there is an Elohim in heaven that revealeth secrets, and maketh known to the king Nebuchadnezzar what shall be in the latter days. Thy dream, and the visions of thy head upon thy bed, are these; as for thee, O king, thy thoughts came into thy mind upon thy bed, what should come to pass hereafter: and he that revealeth secrets maketh known to thee what shall come to pass. But as for me, this secret is not revealed to me for any wisdom that I have more than any living, but for their sakes that shall make known the interpretation to the king, and that thou mightest know the thoughts of thy heart. Thou, O king, sawest, and behold a great image. This great image, whose brightness was excellent, stood before thee; and the form thereof was terrible. This image's head was of fine gold, his breast and his arms of silver, his belly and his thighs of brass, His legs of iron, his feet part of iron and part of clay. Thou sawest till that a **Stone** *was cut out without hands, which smote the image upon his feet that were of iron and clay, and brake them to pieces. Then was the iron, the clay, the brass, the silver, and the gold, broken to pieces together, and became like the chaff of the summer threshing-floors; and the wind carried them away, that no place was found for them: and the stone that smote the image became a great mountain, and filled the whole earth. This is the dream; and we will tell the interpretation thereof before the king. Thou, O king, art a king of kings: for the Elohim of heaven hath given thee a kingdom, power, and strength, and glory. And wheresoever the children of men dwell, the beasts of the field and the fowls of the heaven hath he given into thine hand, and hath made thee ruler over them all. Thou art this head of gold. And after thee shall arise another kingdom inferior to thee, and another third kingdom of brass, which shall bear rule over all the earth. And the fourth kingdom shall be strong as iron: forasmuch as iron breaketh in pieces and subdueth all things: and as iron that breaketh all these, shall it break in pieces and bruise.*

The Mystery of the Cornerstone and the end of the age

Daniel 2, cont,

*And whereas thou sawest the feet and toes, part of potters' clay, and part of iron, the kingdom shall be divided; but there shall be in it of the strength of the iron, forasmuch as thou sawest the iron mixed with miry clay. And as the toes of the feet were part of iron, and part of clay, so the kingdom shall be partly strong, and partly broken. And whereas thou sawest iron mixed with miry clay, they shall mingle themselves with the seed of men: but they shall not cleave one to another, even as iron is not mixed with clay. **And in the days of these kings shall the Elohim of heaven set up a kingdom, which shall never be destroyed: and the kingdom shall not be left to other people, but it shall break in pieces and consume all these kingdoms, and it shall stand for ever. Forasmuch as thou sawest that the <u>Stone</u> <u>was cut out of the mountain without hands</u>, and that it brake in pieces the iron, the brass, the clay, the silver,** and the gold; the great Elohim hath made known to the king what shall come to pass hereafter: and the dream is certain, and the interpretation thereof sure. Then the king Nebuchadnezzar fell upon his face, and worshipped Daniel, and commanded that they should offer an oblation and sweet odors unto him. **The king answered unto Daniel, and said, of a truth it is, that your Elohim is an Elohim of elohim, and a master of kings, and a revealer of secrets, seeing thou couldest reveal this secret.***

May Everything that Has Breath,

May Everything that Has Breath,

May Everything that Has Breath,

May Everything that Has Breath,

Praise ⟨ᴀYᴀZ⟩!

Chapter 4
Remove this Cup from Me!

John 12
[27]"Now I Myself am troubled, and what shall I say? 'Father, save Me from this hour? But for this reason I came to this hour. "Father, esteem Your name." Then a voice came from the heaven, "I have both esteemed it and shall esteem it again."

Knowledge about the real OWYƎZ has been suppressed for hundreds of years. Powerful secular and religious forces rejected the real OWYƎZ long ago. The wicked didn't love OWYƎZ, when He came back then, and the wicked don't love OWYƎZ now. In fact the wicked hate OWYƎZ and ƎYƎZ! The wicked didn't love the things that OWYƎZ said or the things that OWYƎZ did back then because He was a threat to their fat life styles! They didn't love the names of OWYƎZ and ƎYƎZ either, so they tried their best to get rid of those two names! The Roman emperor, Constantine tried to suppress the true nature of Yahushua's sufferings, before His death on the Tree! Instead of the truth, these vipers spawned lies and created an image of a Messiah, who never really even existed! These deceitful men concocted a counterfeit image of OWYƎZ and they even gave OWYƎZ a counterfeit name! These lies have caused billions of hungry sheep to go to their graves being ignorant of the real truth about OWYƎZ! These viper eggs were hatched long ago by Constantine, but they have been perpetuated by the religious institutions of mankind for nearly 1,700 years. We have all greatly misunderstood how much Yahushua really suffered so that Israel could be accepted as sons and daughters into Yahuah's family of elohim! **As you apply the knowledge contained in *Tears in a Bottle* to your own life, please don't let any of Yahushua's tears be wasted!** We all have only one life to live in this present world and we must get it right! Life in this present world is a huge test for each and every one of us! Don't live your whole life concentrating so much on the cares of this world, that you ignore the weightier matters of eternal life! If you miss Yahuah's mark, then you will be ashamed, when you see OWYƎZ face to face! Make the decision to follow Yahushua's narrow Way, even though His way is very afflicted and hard pressed! But in the end, Yahushua's way leads to an eternal life of bliss with OWYƎZ!

Tears in a Bottle

When you are tested in Yahuah's furnace of affliction, **FOLLOW Yahushua's example** for overcoming! If you do, then you won't ever be sorry or ashamed for the decisions that you've made! No, you won't be ashamed; but instead, you will be elated, when you see what OWYƎꟼ has prepared for you! After you read *Tears in a Bottle*, carefully study the Scriptures again in light of your new found understanding. Look for the tears of OWYƎꟼ! Tears that He cried each and every agonizing day during His suffering! You will find that many of the events of Yahushua's life as you previously understood them will take on new meaning! One familiar example is Yahushua's prayer in the Garden just before His arrest! Let's reexamine this familiar story! Everything changes once the sheep understand the truth about OWYƎꟼ and His suffering **before** He hung on the Passover Tree!

Luke 22
[39]*And coming out, He went to the Mount of Olives, according to usage, and His taught ones also followed Him.* [40]*And coming to the place, He said to them, "Pray that you do not enter into trial."* [41]*And He withdrew from them about a stone's throw, and **falling on His knees** He was praying,* [42]*saying, "Father, **if it be Your counsel, remove this cup from Me. Yet not My desire, but let Yours be done."*** [43]***And there appeared a messenger from heaven to Him, strengthening Him.*** [44]***And being <u>in agony</u>, He was praying more earnestly. And His sweat became like <u>great drops of blood falling down to the ground</u>***. [45]*And rising up from prayer, and coming to His taught ones, He found them sleeping from grief.* [46]*And He said to them, "Why do you sleep? Rise and pray, lest you enter into trial."* [47]*And while He was still speaking, see: a crowd! And he who was called Yehudah, one of the twelve, was going before them and came near to* OWYƎꟼ *to kiss Him.* [48]*And* OWYƎꟼ *said to him, "Yehudah, do you deliver up the Son of Adam with a kiss?"*

Mark 14
And OWYƎꟼ *saith unto them, all ye shall be offended because of me this night: for it is written, I will smite the shepherd, and the sheep shall be scattered.*

Mark 14, cont.
*But after that I am risen, I will go before you into Galilee. But Kepha said unto him, although all shall be offended, yet will not I. And OWY3Z saith unto him, verily I say unto thee, that this day, even in this night, before the cock crow twice, thou shalt deny Me thrice. But he spake the more vehemently, if I should die with thee, I will not deny thee in any wise. Likewise also said they all. And they came to a place which was named Gethsemane: and He saith to his disciples, sit ye here, while I shall pray. And He taketh with him Kepha and James and John, and began to be sore amazed, and to be very heavy; And saith unto them, my soul is exceeding __sorrowful unto death__: tarry ye here, and watch. And he went forward a little, **and fell on the ground, and prayed that, if it were possible, the hour might pass from him. And he said, Abba, Father, all things are possible unto thee; __take away this cup from me: nevertheless not what I will, but what thou wilt__**. And he cometh, and findeth them sleeping, and saith unto Kepha, Simon, sleepest thou? Couldest not thou watch one hour? Watch ye and pray, lest ye enter into temptation. The spirit truly is ready, but the flesh is weak. And again He went away, and prayed, and spake the same words. And when He returned, He found them asleep again, (for their eyes were heavy,) and they knew not what to answer him. And He cometh the third time, and saith unto them, sleep on now, and take your rest: it is enough, the hour is come; behold, the Son of man is betrayed into the hands of sinners. Rise up, let us go; lo, he that betrayeth Me is at hand. And immediately, while He yet spake, cometh Judas, one of the twelve, and with him a great multitude with swords and staves, from the chief priests and the scribes and the elders. And He that betrayed him had given them a token, saying, Whomsoever, I shall kiss, that same is he; take him, and lead him away safely. And as soon as He was come, He goeth straightway to him, and saith, Rabbi, Rabbi; and kissed him.*

During His final 3½ years OWY3Z suffered more and more rejections, more and more physical afflictions, and more and more humiliation! On top of all this, there were constant dangers posed by many wicked people wishing to end Yahushua's life! By the end leprosy, the "living death", had transformed Yahushua's face and body into something that no longer even looked human! People were constantly mocking OWY3Z and making jokes about Him! They even put their jokes and taunts to music, which the drunks sang in the streets!

Tears in a Bottle

Everywhere OWY𐤀Z went thousands of people would hide their faces from Him! OWY𐤀Z was rejected from society because of His uncleaness, which resulted from the leprosy that He assimilated as Israel's sin bearer! Leprosy was a penalty imposed on OWY𐤀Z by 𐤀Y𐤀Z for the sins and rebellions of others! OWY𐤀Z felt the full weight of those sins, which were actually the sins of others! Sin terribly vexed Yahushua's spirit! But OWY𐤀Z **became** a sinner because He loved us so much and wanted to please 𐤀Y𐤀Z! OWY𐤀Z **became a sinner, when He carried out His role as Israel's Passover Lamb!** OWY𐤀Z himself said that His sins, **which were actually the sins of others,** numbered more than the hairs on His head! OWY𐤀Z confessed and repented for those sins, **which were actually the sins of others just as we are instructed to do, when we sin!** Each and every day became a torturous struggle for OWY𐤀Z! Some days He would get very, very depressed just like we do! But each and every day OWY𐤀Z trusted in 𐤀Y𐤀Z **for His very survival** that **day**! When He was feeling really, really bad, OWY𐤀Z would often retreat to one of His Mountains to be alone with 𐤀Y𐤀Z and pray! OWY𐤀Z knew that His Father completely understood and would strengthen Him so that He could continue on another day! When the end was near, OWY𐤀Z prayed His famous prayer in the Garden of Gethsemane! When that day came, OWY𐤀Z could hardly even walk anymore! OWY𐤀Z was extremely weak, emaciated, and exhausted! He had very little desire to eat regular food because He was being sustained by spiritual food from 𐤀Y𐤀Z! OWY𐤀Z was bent over and bowed low! He could barely see! It was very difficult for Yahushua to close His eyes, which also made it almost impossible for OWY𐤀Z to sleep! The lesions and sores from the leprosy in Yahushua's body were worm infested, very painful, and smelled awful! Yahushua's bones were disjointed and He spoke of a pain like continuous burning in His loins! OWY𐤀Z specifically noted that His arm was out of joint from His shoulder, so that He could not swing it as He walked! His hands and feet were knurled and disfigured, which made it terribly difficult for OWY𐤀Z to walk! By the end OWY𐤀Z stumbled and trembled like a very old man! His tongue would stick to the roof of His mouth, which made it difficult and painful for OWY𐤀Z to speak! No longer could Yahushua's words flow from His mouth to the poor and needy for hours without end! And finally Yahushua's heart was broken because of the hatred, rejection, greed, violence, and betrayal that were all around Him!

Tears in a Bottle

It was Yahushua's destiny to suffer for His sheep! Near the end, OWYƏZ was experiencing absolute agony and torture every single day! OWYƏZ **was ready for it to be over**! OWYƏZ asked ƏYƏZ to take the cup of His agonizing existence away! Let it be over, but let Yahuah's will be done! OWYƏZ was exhausted and in horrendous agony! Yahushua's will was that the agony of His life would end! Even in His terrible agony, OWYƏZ still elevated His Father's will over His own will! <u>Not</u> my will, but thy will be done! OWYƏZ **was ready to finish His task!** For this I was born! OWYƏZ knew that hanging on the Passover Tree was the last obstacle that He had to overcome, before His mission was finished! OWYƏZ was more than ready for His final test on the Passover Tree!

Thanksgiving Scroll Col 17 1QH
But as for me, from ruin to desolation, from pain to agony, and from travails to torments my soul meditates on your wonders. In your mercy You have not rejected me. Time and time again my soul delights in the abundance of your compassion. I give an answer to those who would wipe me out, and reproof to those who would cast me down. I will condemn his verdict, but Your judgment I honor, for I know Your truth. I shall choose my judgment, and with my agony I am satisfied for I have waited upon Your mercy.

When OWYƏZ prayed in the garden of Gethsemane, **He was <u>not</u> afraid of His death hanging on the Passover Tree because His death would finish everything that OWYƏZ came to do!** Father, mission accomplished! That death on the Passover Tree was the culmination of the mission that ƏYƏZ had sent Him to accomplish, which He alone had to bare! OWYƏZ was ready for the daily cup of agony and misery that He was experiencing to be finished! OWYƏZ was ready for the daily torture that He was experiencing to be completed! OWYƏZ knew that the only thing left was His death on the Passover Tree! OWYƏZ welcomed His end! He knew that His death would herald a new beginning of glory and honor for Himself and all the future overcomers of Israel! HalleluYah! HalleluYah! HalleluYah! What OWYƏZ was asking His Father in the Garden of Gethsemane was for His torturous life in this wicked and depraved world to be finished! But if the timing wasn't in Yahuah's will, then OWYƏZ was prepared to continue on another day! OWYƏZ was ready for closure, but was still completely submissive to Yahuah's will, no matter what!

Tears in a Bottle

But in His mercy and chesed (lovingkindness) **ayal** did answer Yahushua's prayer that night! When **OWYAL** got up from that prayer, He knew that His prayers were answered, when His accusers came to arrest Him!

The inquisition begins!

Matthew 26

[62]And the high priest stood up and said to Him, "Have You no answer to make? What do these witness against You?" [63]But **OWYAL** remained silent. So the high priest said to Him, "I put You to oath, by the living Elohim that You say to us if You are the Messiah, the Son of Elohim." [64] **OWYAL** said to him, "You have said it. Besides I say to you, from now you shall see the Son of Adam sitting at the right hand of the Power, and coming on the clouds of the heaven." [65]Then the high priest tore his garments, saying, "He has blasphemed! Why do we need any more witnesses? See, now you have heard His blasphemy! [66]"What do you think?" And they answering, said, "He is liable to death." [67]**Then they spat in His face and beat Him, and others slapped Him**, [68]saying, **"Prophesy to us, Messiah!** Who is the one who struck You?" [69]And Kepha sat outside in the courtyard, and a servant girl came to him, saying, "And you were with **OWYAL** of Galil." [70]But he denied it before them all, saying, "I do not know what you say." [71]And as he was going out into the porch, another girl saw him and said to those there, "And this one was with **OWYAL** of Natsareth." [72]But again he denied with an oath, "I do not know the Man!" [73]And after a while those who stood by came to him and said to Kepha, "Truly you are one of them too, for even your speech gives you away." [74]Then he began to curse and to swear, saying, "I do not know the Man!" And immediately a cock crowed. [75]And Kepha remembered the word of **OWYAL** who had said to him, "Before a cock crows, you shall deny Me three times." And going out, he wept bitterly.

Matthew 27

And morning having come, all the chief priests and elders of the people took counsel against **OWYAL**, so as to put Him to death. [2]And having bound Him, they led Him away and delivered Him to Pontius Pilate the governor.

Tears in a Bottle

Matthew 27
3 Then Yehudah – he who delivered Him up – having seen that He
had been condemned, repented, returned the thirty pieces of silver to
the chief priests and to the elders, 4 saying, "I have sinned in
delivering up innocent blood." And they said, "What is that to us? You
see to it!" 5 And throwing down the pieces of silver in the Dwelling
Place he left, and went and hanged himself. 6 And the chief priests
took the silver pieces and said, "It is not right to put them into the
treasury, seeing they are the price of blood." 7 So they took counsel
and bought with them the potter's field, for the burial of strangers.
8 Therefore that field has been called the Field of Blood, until today.
9 Then was filled what was spoken by Yirmeyahu the prophet, saying,
"And they took the thirty pieces of silver, the price of Him who was
pierced, on whom they of the children of Yisra'el set a price, 10 and
gave them for the potter's field, as 𐤉𐤄𐤅𐤄 *had ordered me." 11 And*
𐤉𐤄𐤅𐤔𐤏 *stood before the governor, and the governor asked Him,*
saying, "Are You the Sovereign of the Yehudim?" And 𐤉𐤄𐤅𐤔𐤏 *said to*
him, "You say it." 12 And as He was accused by the chief priests and
the elders, He answered not. 13 Then Pilate said to Him, "Do You not
hear how much they witness against You?" 14 And He did not answer
him, not one word, so that the governor wondered much. 15 And at the
festival the governor used to release to the crowd one prisoner whom
they wished. 16 And they had then a well-known prisoner called
Barabba. 17 So when they were assembled, Pilate said to them,
"Whom do you wish I release to you? Barabba, or 𐤉𐤄𐤅𐤔𐤏 *who is*
called Messiah?" 18 For he knew that because of envy they had
delivered Him up. 19 And as he was sitting on the judgment seat, his
wife sent to him, saying, "Have none at all to do with that righteous
Man, for I have suffered much today in a dream because of Him."
20 But the chief priests and elders persuaded the crowds that they
should ask for Barabba and to destroy 𐤉𐤄𐤅𐤔𐤏*. 21 And the governor*
answering, said to them, "Which of the two do you wish I release to
you?" They said, "Barabba!" 22 Pilate said to them, "What then shall I
do with 𐤉𐤄𐤅𐤔𐤏 *who is called Messiah?" They all said to him, "Let Him*
be impaled!" 23 And the governor said, "Indeed, what evil has He
done?" And they were crying out all the more, saying, "Let Him be
impaled!" 24 And when Pilate saw that he was getting nowhere, but
rather an uproar was starting, he took water and washed his hands
before the crowd, saying, "I am innocent of the blood of this
Righteous One. You shall see to it."

Matthew 27, cont.
[25]And all the people answering, said, "His blood be on us and on our children." [26]Then he released Barabba to them, but having OWYƎZ whipped, he delivered Him over to be impaled. [27]Then the soldiers of the governor took OWYƎZ into the court and gathered the entire company of soldiers around Him. [28]And having stripped Him, they put a scarlet robe on Him. [29]And plaiting a crown of thorns, they put it on His head, and a reed in His right hand. **And they kneeled down before Him and mocked Him,** saying, "Greetings, Sovereign of the Yehudim!" [30]**And spitting on Him they took the reed and struck Him on the head.** [31]And when they had mocked Him, they took the robe off Him, then put His own garments on Him, and led Him away to be impaled. [32]And as they were going out, they found a man of Cyrene, Shim'on by name – they compelled him to bear His stake. [33]And when they came to a place called Golgotha, that is to say, Place of a Skull, [34]they gave Him wine mixed with bile to drink. And after tasting, He would not drink it. [35]And having impaled Him, they divided His garments, casting lots, that it might be filled what was spoken by the prophet, "They divided My garments among them, and for My clothing they cast lots." [36]And sitting down, they guarded Him there. [37]And they put up over His head the written charge against Him: THIS IS OWYƎZ, THE SOVEREIGN OF THE YEHUDIM. [38]Then two robbers were impaled with Him, one on the right and another on the left. [39]And those passing by were blaspheming Him, shaking their heads, [40]and saying, "You who destroy the Dwelling Place and build it in three days, save Yourself! If You are the Son of Elohim, come down from the stake."[41]And likewise the chief priests, with the scribes and elders, mocking, said, [42]"He saved others – He is unable to save Himself. If He is the Sovereign of Yisra'el, let Him now come down from the stake, and we shall believe Him. [43]"He trusted in Elohim, let Him rescue Him now if He desires Him, for He said, 'I am the Son of Elohim.' " [44]And also the robbers who were impaled with Him reviled Him, saying the same. [45]And from the sixth hour there was darkness over all the land, until the ninth hour. [46]And about the ninth hour OWYƎZ cried out with a loud voice, saying, "Eli, Eli, lemah shebaqtani?" That is, "My El, My El, why have You forsaken Me?" [47]Some of those standing there, having heard, said, "This One calls Eliyahu!" [48]And immediately one of them ran and took a sponge, and filled it with sour wine and put it on a reed, and gave it to Him to drink.

Matthew 27, cont.
⁴⁹But the rest said, "Leave it, let us see if Eliyahu comes to save Him." ⁵⁰And OWYᗆZ cried out again with a loud voice, and gave up His spirit.

Luke 22
⁵²And OWYᗆZ said to those who had come against Him, the chief priests and captains of the Set-apart Place and the elders, "Have you come out as against a robber, with swords and clubs? ⁵³"While I was with you daily in the Set-apart Place, you did not lay hands on Me. But this is your hour and the authority of darkness." ⁵⁴And having seized Him, they led Him and brought Him to the house of the high priest. And Kepha was following at a distance. ⁵⁵And when they had lit a fire in the midst of the courtyard, and sat down together, Kepha sat among them. ⁵⁶And a certain servant girl, seeing him as he sat by the fire, looked intently at him and said, "And this one was with Him." ⁵⁷But he denied Him, saying, "Woman, I do not know Him." ⁵⁸And after a little while another saw him and said, "You are one of them too." But Kepha said, "Man, I am not!" ⁵⁹And about an hour later, another insisted, saying, "Truly, this one was with Him too, for he is a Galilean too." ⁶⁰But Kepha said, "Man, I do not know what you are saying!" And immediately, while he was still speaking, a cock crowed. ⁶¹And the Master turned and looked at Kepha, and Kepha remembered the word of the Master, how He had said to him, "Before a cock crows, you shall deny Me three times." ⁶²And Kepha went out and wept bitterly. ⁶³And the men who were holding OWYᗆZ were mocking Him, beating Him. **⁶⁴And having blindfolded Him, they were striking Him on the face and were asking Him, saying, "Prophesy! Who is it that struck You?" ⁶⁵And they said to Him much more, blaspheming.**⁶⁶And when it became day, the elders of the people, both chief priests and scribes, came together and they led Him into their council, saying, ⁶⁷"If You are the Messiah, say it to us." And He said to them, "If I say to you, you would not believe it at all, ⁶⁸and if I asked you, you would not answer Me at all. ⁶⁹"From now on the Son of Adam shall sit on the right hand of the power of Elohim." ⁷⁰And they all said, "Are You then the Son of Elohim?" And He said to them, **"You say that I am."** ⁷¹And they said, "Why do we need further witness? For we heard it ourselves from His mouth."

Luke 23
And the entire assembly of them, having risen up, led Him to Pilate, ²and began to accuse Him, saying, "We found this one perverting the nation, and forbidding to pay taxes to Caesar, saying that He Himself is Messiah, a Sovereign." ³And Pilate asked Him, saying, "Are You the Sovereign of the Yehudim?" And answering him He said, "You say it." ⁴And Pilate said to the chief priests and the crowd, "I find no guilt in this Man." ⁵But they were insisting, saying, "He stirs up the people, teaching through all Yehudah, beginning from Galil unto this place." ⁶And when Pilate heard of Galil, he asked if the Man were a Galilean. ⁷And when he learned that He was under the authority of Herodes, he sent Him to Herodes, who was also in Yahrushalayim in those days. ⁸And seeing OWYAZ, Herodes rejoiced greatly, for a long time he had wished to see Him, because he had heard much about Him, and was anticipating to see some miracle done by Him, ⁹and was questioning Him with many words, **but He gave him no answer**. ¹⁰And the chief priests and the scribes stood, accusing Him intensely. ¹¹**And Herodes, with his soldiers, made light of Him and mocked Him**, dressing Him in a splendid robe, and sent Him back to Pilate. ¹²And on that day Pilate and Herodes became friends with each other, for before that they had been at enmity with each other. ¹³And Pilate, having called together the chief priests and the rulers and the people, ¹⁴said to them, "You brought this Man to me, as one who turns away the people. And look, I have examined Him in your presence and have found no guilt in this Man regarding the charges which you make against Him, ¹⁵and neither did Herodes, for I sent you back to him. And look, He has done none at all deserving death. ¹⁶"Having disciplined Him, then, I shall release Him" – ¹⁷for he had to release one to them at the festival. ¹⁸And they cried out, all together, saying, "Away with this One, and release to us Barabba" ¹⁹(who had been thrown into prison for a certain uprising made in the city, and for murder). ²⁰Wishing to release OWYAZ, then, Pilate appealed to them again. ²¹But they were calling out, saying, "Impale! Impale Him!" ²²And he said to them the third time, "Why, what evil has He done? I have found no reason for death in Him. Having disciplined Him then, I shall release Him." ²³But with loud voices they insisted, asking for Him to be impaled. And the voices of these men and of the chief priests were prevailing. ²⁴And Pilate pronounced sentence that what they asked should be done.

Luke 23, cont.
[25]*And he released the one they asked for, who for uprising and murder had been thrown into prison, but he handed* OWYƷZ *over to their wishes.* [26]*And as they led Him away, they laid hold of a certain man, Shim'on a Cyrenian, who was coming from the field, and they put the stake on him, to bear it behind* OWYƷZ. [27]*And a great number of the people were following Him, and women who also were mourning and lamenting Him.* [28]*But* OWYƷZ, *turning to them, said, "Daughters of Yahrushalayim, do not weep for Me, but weep for yourselves and for your children.* [29]*"For look, days are coming in which they shall say, 'Blessed are the barren, and wombs that never bore, and the breasts which never nursed!'* [30]*"Then they shall begin to say to the mountains, "Fall on us!" and to the hills, "Cover us!" '* [31]*"Because if they do this to the green tree, what is going to be done to the dry tree?"* [32]*And two others also, evil-doers, were led with Him to be put to death.* [33]*And when they had come to the place called Golgotha, they impaled Him there, and the evil-doers, one on the right and the other on the left.* [34]*And* OWYƷZ *said, "Father, forgive them, for they do not know what they do." And they divided His garments and cast lots.* [35]*And the people were standing, looking on, and the rulers also were sneering with them, saying, "He saved others, let Him save Himself if He is the Messiah, the chosen of Elohim."* [36]*And the soldiers were mocking Him too, coming and offering Him sour wine,* [37]*and saying, "If You are the Sovereign of the Yehudim, save Yourself."* [38]*And there was also an inscription written over Him in letters of Greek, and Roman, and Hebrew: THIS IS THE SOVEREIGN OF THE YEHUDIM.* [39]*And one of the evil-doers who were hanged, was speaking evil of Him, saying, "If You are the Messiah, save Yourself and us."* [40]*But the other, responding, rebuked him, saying, "Do you not even fear Elohim, since you are under the same judgment?* [41]*"And we, indeed, rightly so, for we receive the due reward of our deeds, but this One has done no wrong."* [42]*And he said to* OWYƷZ, *"Master, remember me when You come into Your reign."* [43]*And* OWYƷZ *aid to him, "Truly, I say to you today, you shall be with Me in Paradise."* [44]***And it was now about the sixth hour and darkness came over all the land, until the ninth hour.*** [45]***And the sun was darkened, and the veil of the Dwelling Place was torn in two.*** [46]***And crying out with a loud voice,*** OWYƷZ ***said, "Father, into Your hands I commit My spirit." And having said this, He breathed His last.***

Luke 23, cont.
⁴⁷And the captain, seeing what took place, praised Elohim, saying, "Truly, this Man was righteous!" ⁴⁸*And when all the crowds who had gathered to that sight saw what took place, they beat their breasts and went away.*

It was the dream of His future glory with ᴀYᴀ꒒ and the Righteous of Israel that kept OWYᴀ꒒ going! OWYᴀ꒒ knew Yahuah's truth and that truth kept Yahushua's eyes focused on His mission and **not** on the retched condition of His existence! **Israel shall walk by faith and not by sight!** OWYᴀ꒒ surely came in the flesh and was tested in Yahuah's furnace of affliction, but OWYᴀ꒒ did not personally sin, ever! **OWYᴀ꒒ literally bore the sins of others in His body of flesh!** All of our sins and their penalties were counted to Yahushua's account, not ours, **if we follow His narrow way**!

John 18 The Passover Tree!
²⁸*Then they led* OWYᴀ꒒ *from Qayapha to the palace, and it was early. And they themselves did not go into the palace, lest they should be defiled, but that they might eat the Passover.* ²⁹*Pilate, therefore, came out to them and said, "What accusation do you bring against this Man?"* ³⁰*They answered and said to him, "If He were not an evil-doer, we would not have delivered Him up to you."* ³¹*Then Pilate said to them, "You take Him and judge Him according to your law." The Yehudim said to him, "It is not right for us to put anyone to death,"* ³²*in order that the word of* OWYᴀ꒒ *might be filled which He spoke, signifying by what death He was about to die.* ³³*Then Pilate went back into the palace, and called* OWYᴀ꒒*, and said to Him, "Are You the Sovereign of the Yehudim?"* ³⁴OWYᴀ꒒ *answered him, "Do you say this from yourself, or did others talk to you about Me?"* ³⁵*Pilate answered, "Am I a Yehudite? Your own nation and the chief priests have delivered You to me. What did You do?"* ³⁶OWYᴀ꒒ *answered, "My reign is not of this world. If My reign were of this world, My servants would fight, so that I should not be delivered to the Yehudim. But now My reign is not from here."* ³⁷*Then Pilate said to Him, "You are a sovereign, then?"* OWYᴀ꒒ *answered, "You say it, because I am a sovereign. For this I was born, and for this I have come into the world, that I should bear witness to the truth. Everyone who is of the truth hears My voice."* ³⁸*Pilate said to Him, "What is truth?" And when he had said this, he went out again to the Yehudim, and said to them, "I find no guilt in Him.*

John 18, cont.
[39]"But you have a habit that I shall release someone to you at the Passover. Do you wish, then, that I release to you the Sovereign of the Yehudim?" [40]Then they all shouted again, saying, "Not this One, but Barabba!" And Barabba was a robber.

John 19
Then, therefore, Pilate took OWYƎZ and flogged Him. [2]And the soldiers plaited a crown of thorns and placed it on His head, and they put a purple robe on Him, [3]and came to Him and said, "Greetings, Sovereign of the Yehudim!" And they slapped Him in the face. [4]And Pilate went outside again, and said to them, "See, I am bringing Him out to you, to let you know that I find no guilt in Him." [5]Then OWYƎZ came outside, wearing the crown of thorns and the purple robe. And Pilate said to them, "See the Man!" [6]So when the chief priests and officers saw Him, they shouted, saying, "Impale! Impale!" Pilate said to them, "You take Him and impale Him, for I find no guilt in Him." [7]The Yehudim answered him, "We have a law, and according to our law He ought to die, for He has made Himself the Son of Elohim." [8]So when Pilate heard this word, he was more afraid, [9]and went back into the palace, and asked OWYƎZ, "Where are You from?" But OWYƎZ gave him no answer. [10]Then Pilate said to Him, "Do You not speak to me? Do You not know that I possess authority to impale You, and I possess authority to release You?" [11]OWYƎZ answered, "You would possess no authority against Me if it were not given you from above. Because of this, he who delivered Me to you has greater sin." [12]From then on Pilate was seeking to release Him, but the Yehudim shouted, saying, "If you release this One, you are not Caesar's friend. Everyone who makes himself a sovereign, does speak against Caesar." [13]Therefore, when Pilate heard these words, he brought OWYƎZ out and sat down in the judgment seat in a place that is called Pavement, but in Hebrew, Gabbatha. [14]And it was the Preparation Day of the Passover week, and about the sixth hour. And he said to the Yehudim, "See your Sovereign!" [15]But they shouted, "Away, away, impale Him!" Pilate said to them, "Shall I impale your Sovereign?" The chief priests answered, "We have no sovereign except Caesar!" [16]At that time, then, he delivered Him to them to be impaled. And they took OWYƎZ and led Him away. [17]And bearing His stake, He went out to the so-called Place of a Skull, which is called in Hebrew, Golgotha, [18]where they impaled Him, and two others with Him, one on this side and one on that side, and OWYƎZ in the middle.

John 19, cont.
[19]*And Pilate wrote a title too, and put it on the stake, and it was written:* OWYƎZ *OF NATSARETH, THE SOVEREIGN OF THE YEHUDIM.* [20]*Many of the Yehudim therefore read this title, for the place where* OWYƎZ *as impaled was near the city, and it was written in Hebrew, in Greek, in Roman.* [21]*So the chief priests of the Yehudim said to Pilate, "Do not write, 'The Sovereign of the Yehudim,' but, 'He said, "I am the Sovereign of the Yehudim." ' "* [22]*Pilate answered, "What I have written, I have written."* [23]*Then the soldiers, when they had impaled* OWYƎZ*, took His outer garments and made four parts, to each soldier a part, and the inner garment. But the inner garment was without seam, woven from the top in one piece.* [24]*So they said to each other, "Let us not tear it, but cast lots for it – whose it shall be," in order that the Scripture might be filled which says, "They divided My garments among them, and for My clothing they cast lots." The soldiers therefore indeed did this.* [25]*And by the stake of* OWYƎZ *stood His mother, and His mother's sister, Miryam the wife of Qlophah, and Miryam from Magdala.* [26]*Then* OWYƎZ*, seeing His mother and the taught one whom He loved standing by, He said to His mother, "Woman, see your son!"* [27]*Then to the taught one He said, "See, your mother!" And from that hour that taught one took her to his own home.* [28]*After this,* OWYƎZ*, knowing that all had been accomplished, in order that the Scripture might be accomplished, said, "I thirst!"* [29]*A bowl of sour wine stood there, and they filled a sponge with sour wine, put it on hyssop, and held it to His mouth.* [30]*So when* OWYƎZ *took the sour wine He said, "It has been accomplished!" And bowing His head, He gave up His spirit.* [31]*Therefore, since it was the Preparation Day, that the bodies should not remain on the stake on the Sabbath – for that Sabbath was a high one – the Yehudim asked Pilate to have their legs broken, and that they be taken away.* [32]*Therefore the soldiers came and broke the legs of the first, and of the other who was impaled with Him,* [33]*but when they came to* OWYƎZ *and saw that He was already dead, they did not break His legs.* [34]*But one of the soldiers pierced His side with a spear, and instantly blood and water came out.*

In those days the real OWYƎZ was despised and rejected more than any man on earth! Today the real OWYƎZ **is <u>still</u> despised more than any man on earth**! And just as it was in that day, today the religious authorities and institutions are still Yahushua's #1 nemesis! The real OWYƎZ polarizes people today just like He did back then!

Tears in a Bottle

Summary

Only a remnant of called out ones have eyes that really see and ears that really hear! They are the chosen of 𐤀𐤉𐤄𐤆! Sadly most morally good people today love the lies of tradition more than they love the truth of 𐤀𐤉𐤄𐤆! These blinded sheep love the lies of apostasy more than Yahuah's truth! So they ignore the call of 𐤀𐤉𐤄𐤆! In His misery and anguish OWYƎZ **still followed the Torah** and did only good as He helped the poor and needy of this world! OWYƎZ ministered and served the poor and needy, **until He physically could not go anymore**! OWYƎZ was afflicted by horrendous sicknesses and diseases to the point where He was no longer recognizable as a human being! But all this OWYƎZ bore because of His infinite mercy, compassion, and loving-kindness towards you and me! The people of Israel did not esteem Him, but they deemed OWYƎZ stricken and cursed, a vessel to be discarded! **The curse OWYƎZ bore was not for His own sins, but for my sins and your sins**! Back then the sheep were **offended** by Yahushua's horrendous outward physical appearance! As a result, OWYƎZ became **the stumbling block** in this wicked world, which men have wrestled with and stumbled over for nearly 2,000 years! OWYƎZ has become Yahuah's chief cornerstone and Israel's High priest in the order of Malkitsedeq, before the throne of 𐤀𐤉𐤄𐤆!

HalleluYah! HalleluYah!

HalleluYah!

Baruch 𐤀𐤉𐤄𐤆

Chapter 5
Have You Seen Him?

On my bed at night I sought the beloved of my being; I sought him, but I did not find him. [2]"Come, let me arise, and go about the city, in the streets and in the broad places I seek the beloved of my being." I sought him, but I did not find him. [3]The watchmen who go about the city found me, to whom I said, "Have you seen the beloved of my being?" Shir HaShirim (Song of Songs) 3

Why couldn't Mary and the disciples recognize OWYƷZ, after His resurrection? Why was it so difficult? Hadn't it only been three days, since OWYƷZ was buried? What had changed? Weren't His disciples extremely familiar with Yahushua's appearance? After all, hadn't they traveled and sojourned across the land of Israel with OWYƷZ for nearly three years? So what was the problem? Mary and Yahushua's disciples were very familiar with Yahushua's diseased, emaciated, and leprous appearance! When OWYƷZ was resurrected, He looked like someone else, not the OWYƷZ **they knew so well**! Mary and the disciples were confused and taken back, when OWYƷZ appeared to them in a body that was not cursed, leprous, diseased, or emaciated! That's why they didn't recognize OWYƷZ! **Yahushua's appearance was no longer grotesque, contemptible, loathsome, and unclean!** The change in Yahushua's appearance was in such stark contrast that it was mind boggling to them! It was like they were dreaming!

Luke 24

And on the first day of the week, at early dawn, they came to the tomb, bringing the spices which they had prepared, [2]and they found the stone rolled away from the tomb. [3]And having entered, they did not find the body of the Master OWYƷZ. [4]And it came to be, as they were perplexed about this, that see, two men stood by them in glittering garments. [5]And becoming frightened and bowing their faces to the earth, these said to them, "Why do you seek the living among the dead? [6]"He is not here, but has been raised up! Remember how He spoke to you when He was still in Galil, [7]saying, 'The Son of Adam has to be delivered into the hands of sinners, and be impaled, and the third day rise again.' " [8]And they remembered His words.

Luke 24, cont.

⁹*And having returned from the tomb they reported all this to the eleven and to all the rest.* ¹⁰*And it was Miryam from Magdala, and Yohanah, and Miryam the mother of Ya'aqob, and the rest with them, who told this to the emissaries.* ¹¹*And their words appeared to them to be nonsense, and they did not believe them.* ¹²*But Kepha arose and ran to the tomb. And stooping down, he saw the linen wrappings lying by themselves. And he went away home, marveling at what took place.* ¹³**And see, two of them were going that same day to a village called Amma'us, which was twelve kilometers from Yahrushalayim.** ¹⁴**And they were talking to each other of all this which had taken place.** ¹⁵**And it came to be, as they were talking and reasoning, that OWYAZ Himself drew near and went with them.** ¹⁶**But their eyes were restrained, so that they did not know Him.** ¹⁷*And He said to them, "What are these words you are exchanging with each other as you are walking – and you are sad?"* ¹⁸*And the one whose name was Qleophas answering, said to Him, "Are You the lone visitor in Yahrushalayim who does not know what took place in it these days?"* ¹⁹*And He said to them, "What?" And they said to Him, "Concerning OWYAZ of Natsareth, who was a Prophet mighty in deed and word before Elohim and all the people,* ²⁰*and how the chief priests and our rulers delivered Him to be condemned to death, and impaled Him.* ²¹*"We, however, were expecting that it was He who was going to redeem Yisra'el. But besides all this, today is the third day since these matters took place. arrived at the tomb early, also astonished us,* ²³*when they did not find His body, they came saying that they had also seen a vision of messengers who said He was alive.* ²⁴*"And some of those with us went to the tomb and found it, as also the women had said, but they did not see Him."* ²⁵*And He said to them, "O thoughtless ones, and slow of heart to believe in all that the prophets have spoken!* ²⁶*"Was it not necessary for the Messiah to suffer these and to enter into His esteem?"* ²⁷**And beginning at Mosheh and all the Prophets, He was explaining to them in all the Scriptures the matters concerning Himself.** ²⁸*And they approached the village where they were going, and He seemed to be going on.* ²⁹*But they urged Him strongly, saying, "Stay with us, for it is toward evening, and the day has declined." And He went in to stay with them.* ³⁰*And it came to be, when He sat at the table with them, having taken the bread, He blessed, and having broken, He was giving it to them.*

Luke 24, cont.
³¹And their eyes were opened and they recognized Him. *And He disappeared from their sight.* ³²*And they said to each other, "Was not our heart burning within us as He was speaking to us on the way, and as He was opening the Scriptures to us?"* ³³*And rising up that same hour they returned to Yahrushalayim, and found the eleven and those who were with them gathered together,* ³⁴*saying, "The Master was truly raised, and has appeared to Shim'on!"* ³⁵*And they related what took place on the way, and how He was recognized by them in the breaking of the bread.* ³⁶*And as they were saying this,* OWYƎZ *Himself stood in the midst of them, and said to them, "Peace to you."* ³⁷*And being startled and frightened, they thought they had seen a spirit.* ³⁸*And He said to them, "Why are you troubled? And why do doubts arise in your hearts?* ³⁹*"See My hands and My feet, that it is I Myself. Handle Me and see, for a spirit does not have flesh and bones as you see I have."* ⁴⁰*And saying this, He showed them His hands and His feet.* ⁴¹*And while they were still not believing for joy, and marveling, He said to them, "Have you any food here?"* ⁴²*And they gave Him a piece of a broiled fish and some honeycomb.* ⁴³*And taking it He ate in their presence.* ⁴⁴*And He said to them, "These are the words which I spoke to you while I was still with you, that all have to be filled that were written in the Torah of Mosheh and the Prophets and the Psalms concerning Me."* ⁴⁵*Then He opened their minds to understand the Scriptures,* ⁴⁶*and said to them, "Thus it has been written, and so it was necessary for the Messiah to suffer and to rise again from the dead the third day,* ⁴⁷*and that repentance and forgiveness of sins should be proclaimed in His Name to all nations, beginning at Yahrushalayim.*

John 20
And on the first day of the week Miryam from Magdala came early to the tomb, while it was still dark, and saw that the stone had been removed from the tomb. ²*So she ran and came to Shim'on Kepha, and to the other taught one whom* OWYƎZ *loved, and said to them, "They have taken the Master out of the tomb, and we do not know where they laid Him."* ³*Then Kepha and the other taught one went out, and they were going to the tomb,* ⁴*and the two were running together, but the other taught one outran Kepha and came to the tomb first.* ⁵*And stooping down he saw the linen wrappings lying, but he did not go in.*

Tears in a Bottle

John 20, cont.
⁶Then Shim'on Kepha came, following him, and went into the tomb. And he saw the linen wrappings lying, ⁷and the cloth which had been on His head, not lying with the linen wrappings, but folded up in a place by itself. ⁸So, then, the other taught one, who came to the tomb first, also went in. And he saw and believed. ⁹For they did not yet know the Scripture, that He has to rise again from the dead. ¹⁰Therefore the taught ones went away again, by themselves. **¹¹But Miryam was standing outside by the tomb weeping. Then as she wept, she stooped down to the tomb, ¹²and saw two messengers in white sitting, one at the head and the other at the feet, where the body of OWYƎZ had been laid. ¹³And they said to her, "Woman, why do you weep?" She said to them, "Because they took away my Master, and I do not know where they laid Him."** ¹⁴And having said this, <u>she turned around and saw OWYƎZ standing, but she did not know that it was OWYƎZ.</u> ¹⁵OWYƎZ said to her, "Woman, why do you weep? Whom do you seek?" <u>Thinking He was the gardener,</u> she said to Him, "Master, if You have carried Him away, say to me where You put Him, and I shall take Him away." ¹⁶<u>OWYƎZ said to her, "Miryam!" She turned and said to Him, "Rabboni!" (which means Teacher).</u> ¹⁷OWYƎZ said to her, "Do not hold on to Me, for I have not yet ascended to My Father. But go to My brothers and say to them, 'I am ascending to My Father and your Father, and to My Elohim and your Elohim.' " ¹⁸Miryam from Magdala came announcing to the taught ones that she had seen the Master, and that He had told her this.*
¹⁹When therefore it was evening on that day, the first day of the week, and when the doors were shut where the taught ones met, for fear of the Yehudim, OWYƎZ came and stood in the midst, and said to them, "Peace to you." ²⁰And having said this, He showed them His hands and His side. The taught ones therefore rejoiced when they saw the Master. ²¹Then OWYƎZ said to them again, "Peace to you! As the Father has sent Me, I also send you." ²²And having said this, He breathed on them, and said to them, "Receive the Set-apart Spirit. ²³"If you forgive the sins of any, they are forgiven them; if you retain the sins of any, they have been retained."

John 20, cont.
[24]*But T'oma, called the Twin, one of the twelve, was not with them when* OWYƐZ *came,* [25]*so the other taught ones said to him, "We have seen the Master." But he said to them,* **"Unless I see in His hands the mark of the nails, and put my finger into the imprint of the nails, and put my hand into His side, I shall by no means believe."** [26]**And after eight days His taught ones were again inside, and T'oma with them.** OWYƐZ **came**, *the doors having been shut, and He stood in the midst, and said, "Peace to you!"* [27]*Then He said to T'oma, "Bring your finger here, and see My hands. And bring your hand and put it into My side – and do not be unbelieving, but believing."* [28]*And T'oma answered and said to Him, "My Master and my Elohim!"* [29] OWYƐZ *said to him, "T'oma, because you have seen Me, you have believed.* **Blessed are those who have not seen and have believed."** [30]*There were indeed many other signs that* OWYƐZ *did in the presence of His taught ones, which are not written in this book,* [31]*but these have been written so that you believe that* OWYƐZ *is the Messiah, the Son of Elohim, and that, believing,* **you might possess life in His Name**. *(The knowledge and love for the names of* OWYƐZ *and* ƐYƐZ *are vital to your eternal life! Selah!)*

John 21
After this OWYƐZ *manifested Himself again to the taught ones at the Sea of Kinnereth, and He manifested this way:* [2]*Shim'on Kepha, and T'oma called the Twin, and Nethane'l of Qanah in Galil, the sons of Zabdai, and two others of His taught ones were together.* [3]*Shim'on Kepha said to them, "I am going to fish." They said to him, "We are also coming with you." They went out and immediately entered into the boat. And that night they caught none at all.* [4]*But when it became early morning,* OWYƐZ *stood on the beach.* **However, the taught ones did not know that it was** OWYƐZ. [5]*Then* OWYƐZ *said to them, "Children, have you any food?" They answered Him, "No."* [6]*And He said to them, "Throw the net on the right side of the boat, and you shall find." So they threw, and they were no longer able to draw it in because of the large number of fish.* [7]*That taught one whom* OWYƐZ *loved then said to Kepha, "It is the Master!" Then Shim'on Kepha, hearing that it was the Master, put on his outer garment – for he was stripped – and plunged into the sea.*

John 21, cont.

[8]And the other taught ones came in the little boat – for they were not far from land, but about two hundred cubits – dragging the net with fish. [9]So when they had come to land, they saw a fire of coals there, and fish laid on it, and bread. [10] OWY3Z said to them, "Bring some of the fish which you have now caught." [11]Shim'on Kepha went up and dragged the net to land, filled with one hundred and fifty-three big fishes. And though there were so many, the net was not broken. [12] OWY3Z said to them, "Come, have breakfast." And not one of the taught ones had the courage to ask Him, "Who are You?," knowing that it was the Master. [13] OWY3Z came and took the bread and gave it to them, and the same with the fish.[14]**This was now the third time OWY3Z was manifested to His taught ones after He was raised from the dead.**

Matthew 18

But if he will not hear thee, then take with thee one or two more, that **in the mouth of two or three witnesses every word may be established.**

What was the reason that Mary and the disciples had such difficulty recognizing OWY3Z, when they saw Him, after His resurrection? Now you know the answer lies with their familiarity with Yahushua's former loathsome appearance! They had forgotten or maybe they had never known what OWY3Z actually looked like, before OWY3Z became afflicted with leprosy and the other wasting diseases!

Chapter 6
Overcome with 𐤀Y𐤀Z!

[28]And He said, "Your name is no longer called Ya'aqob, but Yisra'el, because you have striven with Elohim and with men, and have OVERCOME." Bereshith (*Genesis*) 32

To be victorious, it is imperative that Israel follow Yahushua's pattern for overcoming the struggles and afflictions that they will face in their lives! Israel **will** be put in Yahuah's furnace of affliction to be tested because that's the way 𐤀Y𐤀Z has willed it! 𐤀Y𐤀Z has determined that all those, who have **accepted** His call on their lives, will be tested in His crucible of affliction. The called out ones, who 𐤀Y𐤀Z loves as sons and daughters, will be tested and purified to perfection, much the same as gold and silver are perfected in the heat of a furnace. The hotter the fire, the more the impurities will be burnt off! Eventually only precious metal is left! So it is in my life and so it has been throughout all the generations of Israel! 𐤀Y𐤀Z does **not** test the people called Israel because He wants to destroy them, but 𐤀Y𐤀Z tests Israel because He loves them so much! 𐤀Y𐤀Z created Israel to be set apart vessels for Himself. 𐤀Y𐤀Z knows exactly what has to be done in the lives of Israel to transform each and every one into the image of OWY𐤀Z! Sometimes we cannot see or understand, but in the end, **if we patiently endure as OWY𐤀Z endured, then all our questions will be answered and we will be satisfied with the result**! We will **not** be sorry for following OWY𐤀Z! 𐤀Y𐤀Z uses struggles and extreme hardships in this life to make huge refinements in our character for eternity! The struggles are the catalysts that 𐤀Y𐤀Z uses to humble Israel and to draw Israel to Himself! Remember 𐤀Y𐤀Z **is the master potter and we are His clay**! Who are we to question His methods?

Romans 8
The Spirit itself beareth witness with our spirit, that we are the children of 𐤀Y𐤀Z: And if children, then heirs; heirs of 𐤀Y𐤀Z, and joint-heirs with the Messiah; if so be that we suffer with him, that we may be also glorified together. For I reckon that the sufferings of this present time are not worthy to be compared with the glory which shall be revealed in us. For the earnest expectation of the creature waiteth for the manifestation of the sons of 𐤀Y𐤀Z.

Tears in a Bottle

Romans 8, cont.

*For the creature was made subject to vanity, not willingly, but by reason of him who hath subjected the same in hope, because the creature itself also shall be delivered from the bondage of corruption into the glorious liberty of the children of ﭏﭏﭏ. For we know that the whole creation groaneth and travaileth in pain together until now. And not only they, but ourselves also, which have the first fruits of the Spirit, even we ourselves groan within ourselves, waiting for the adoption, to wit, the redemption of our body. For we are saved by hope: but hope that is seen is not hope: for what a man seeth, why doth he yet hope for? But if we hope for that we see not, then do we with patience wait for it. Likewise **the Spirit also helpeth our infirmities**: for we know not what we should pray for as we ought: but the Spirit itself maketh intercession for us with groanings which cannot be uttered. And he that searcheth the hearts knoweth what is the mind of the Spirit, because he maketh intercession for the saints according to the will of ﭏﭏﭏ. And **we know that all things work together for good** to them that love ﭏﭏﭏ, to them **who are the called** according to his purpose. For whom he did foreknow, **he also did predestinate** to be **conformed to the image of his Son**, that he might be **the firstborn among many brethren**. Moreover whom he did predestinate, them he also called: and whom he called, them he also justified: and whom he justified, them **he also glorified**. What shall we then say to these things? If ﭏﭏﭏ be for us, who can be against us? He that spared not his own Son, but delivered him up for us all, how shall he not with him also freely give us all things? Who shall lay any thing to the charge of Yahuah's elect? It is ﭏﭏﭏ that justifieth. Who is he that condemneth? It is the Messiah that died, yea rather, that is risen again, who is even at the right hand of ﭏﭏﭏ, who also maketh intercession for us. Who shall separate us from the love of the Messiah? Shall tribulation, or distress, or persecution, or famine, or nakedness, or peril, or sword? As it is written, for thy sake we are killed all the day long; we are accounted as sheep for the slaughter. nay, in all these things **we are more than conquerors through him that loved us.** For I am persuaded, that neither death, nor life, nor angels, nor principalities, nor powers, nor things present, nor things to come, nor height, nor depth, nor any other creature, shall be able to separate us from the love of ﭏﭏﭏ, which is in Messiah OWﭏﭏﭏ our Savior.*

Tears in a Bottle

When a person, who ayaz calls is totally humbled, then they become **really hungry to learn the Truth**! For Israel the pursuit of wisdom and understanding is a matter of life and death! The overcomers of Israel are on a quest to discover Yahuah's Truth! The people of ayaz develop an extreme love for the truth as well as a complete **disgust** for the lies that previously enslaved them! Israel will be led by Yahuah's Ruach HaQodesh to go back to the old ways and to discover things that have been lost and hidden in the religious traditions of mankind for a very long time! And Israel will discover a great love for the Torah! Then they will begin to understand what righteousness is all about! Over time the overcomers, who ayaz calls Israel, will make a lot of changes in their lives in order to align themselves **perfectly** with Yahuah's Torah! **The goal is to be judged with a perfect heart just like David, Noah, Daniel, Adam, Seth, Enoch, and the myriads of the elect of Israel! Very early in their journey, the called out ones will begin to experience troubles, hardships, and afflictions as they are placed in Yahuah's furnace of affliction! These troubles will escalate at an alarming rate! Israel will experience rejection and often some form of persecution and betrayal from family and close friends! And then of course there's the constant oppression from the outright wicked!** Don't forget about them! The wicked won't like the people of Israel from the very first time they lay their eyes on you! It's innate, so don't be surprised! And Israel won't like them either! It's the contrast between the East and the West or Light and Darkness! It's just the way things are! Israel will mourn for the condition of this world and the deception that has trapped so many morally good people! Israel's chief desire will be the return of OWYAZ and the establishment of His kingdom! Our Father, who inhabits the Heavens, Set Apart is your name (ayaz)! May Your Kingdom come and Your will be done on earth as it is in the Heavens!

Hebrews 10
*But call to remembrance the former days, in which, **after ye were illuminated, ye endured a great fight of afflictions**; Partly, whilst ye were made a gazing stock both by **reproaches** and **afflictions**; and partly, whilst ye became companions of them that were so used. **For ye had compassion of me in my bonds, and took joyfully the spoiling of your goods, knowing in yourselves that ye have in heaven a better and an enduring substance.** Cast not away therefore your confidence, which hath great recompense of reward.*

Hebrews 10, cont.
For ye have need of <u>patience</u>, that, after ye have done the will of 𐤉𐤄𐤅𐤄, ye might receive the promise. For yet a little while, and he that shall come will come, and will not tarry. Now the just shall live by faith: but if any man draw back, my soul shall have no pleasure in him. But we are not of them who draw back unto perdition; but of them that believe to the saving of the soul.

𐤉𐤄𐤅𐤄 has ordained that His called out ones **<u>will</u>** follow in the footsteps of 𐤉𐤄𐤅𐤔𐤏! They will experience the same types of struggles that 𐤉𐤄𐤅𐤔𐤏 experienced, but of course in much smaller degrees! 𐤉𐤄𐤅𐤔𐤏 experienced increditable struggles, afflictions, and rejections, while He was on the earth and His called out ones should expect to experience those types of things too, **but of course in much smaller doses**! 𐤉𐤄𐤅𐤔𐤏 overcame them all by the power of 𐤉𐤄𐤅𐤄 and the remnant of Israel will do the same thing! 𐤉𐤄𐤅𐤔𐤏 suffered all His agonies without complaining or turning away from His appointed mission! 𐤉𐤄𐤅𐤔𐤏 was the consummate suffering servant of 𐤉𐤄𐤅𐤄 and He was a <u>model</u> son! 𐤉𐤄𐤅𐤔𐤏 is our savior and our example for patient endurance in this world! If you truly love 𐤉𐤄𐤅𐤔𐤏 and want to follow His narrow Way, then you **<u>must follow Yahushua's lead</u>**! You must be willing to suffer and endure all types of hardships in Yahushua's name!

Matthew 10:39 *He that findeth his life shall lose it: and he that loseth his life for my sake shall find it.*

Matthew 16:25 *For whosoever will save his life shall lose it: and whosoever will lose his life for my sake shall find it.*

Mark 8:35 *For whosoever will save his life shall lose it; but whosoever shall lose his life for my sake and the gospel's, the same shall save it.*

Luke 9:24 *For whosoever will save his life shall lose it: but whosoever will lose his life for my sake, the same shall save it.*

Luke 17:33 *Whosoever shall seek to save his life shall lose it; and whosoever shall lose his life shall preserve it.*

John 12:25 *He that loveth his life shall lose it; and he that hateth his life in this world shall keep it unto life eternal.*

May 𐤉𐤄𐤅𐤄 give you His wisdom, His understanding, and His insight in the midst of all your personal struggles! If you are sincere, then 𐤉𐤄𐤅𐤄 will carry you through them all just like 𐤉𐤄𐤅𐤄 has carried the remnant of Israel throughout every generation! Many are the afflictions of the Righteous, but 𐤉𐤄𐤅𐤄 carries His children through them all!

Tears in a Bottle

When you determine to follow OWYƎZ, it will take great courage! It will involve many personal changes in the short term! Your race will be a race of patient endurance! **Yahushua's Way is a very hard and afflicted way because it involves so many troubles and so many afflictions**! Few choose to travel Yahushua's Way because **it's hard**! But of course, the way leading to destruction is **very easy** and many go that way!

2 Corinthians
We are troubled on every side, yet not distressed; we are perplexed, but not in despair; Persecuted, but not forsaken; cast down, but not destroyed; always bearing about in the body the dying of the Master OWYƎZ, that the life also of OWYƎZ might be made manifest in our body. For we which live are always delivered unto death for OWYƎZ sake, that the life also of OWYƎZ might be made manifest in our mortal flesh. So then death worketh in us, but life in you. We having the same spirit of faith, according as it is written, I believed, and therefore have I spoken; we also believe, and therefore speak; knowing that he which raised up the Master OWYƎZ shall raise up us also by OWYƎZ, and shall present us with you. For all things are for your sakes, that the abundant favor might through the thanksgiving of many redound to the glory of ƎYƎZ. For which cause we faint not; but though our outward man perish, yet the inward man is renewed day by day. For our light affliction, which is but for a moment, worketh for us a far more exceeding and eternal weight of glory; While we look not at the things which are seen, but at the things which are not seen: for the things which are seen are temporal; but the things which are not seen are eternal.

1Peter 1 That the trial of your faith, being much more precious than of gold that perisheth, though it be tried with fire, might be found unto praise and honor and glory at the appearing of OWYƎZ the Messiah: whom having not seen you love. Though now you do not see Him, yet believing, you rejoice with joy inexpressible and full of glory, receiving the end of your faith-the salvation of your souls. Of this salvation the prophets have inquired and searched carefully, who prophesied of the favor that would come to you, searching what, or what manner of time, the Spirit of the Messiah who was in them was indicating when He testified beforehand the sufferings of the Messiah and the glories that would follow.

1 Peter 4
Beloved, think it not strange concerning the fiery trial which is to try you, as though some strange thing happened unto you: But rejoice, inasmuch as ye are partakers of Messiah's sufferings; that, when his glory shall be revealed, ye may be glad also with exceeding joy.

The Davidic Psalms were written so that all the future generations of Israel could hear the very heartbeat of OWYƎⱫ! In the Davidic Psalms OWYƎⱫ speaks from the first person perspective concerning His sufferings, His dreams, and His secrets for overcoming! These Psalms as well as the Thanksgiving Scrolls give Israel insight into Yahushua's heart and what OWYƎⱫ was experiencing as His ministry progressed day to day! Yahushua's horrible sufferings as well as Yahushua's thoughts, desires, and dreams were recorded for all the future generations of Israel **to see, to think about, and to unite with**! What exactly did OWYƎⱫ mean in Matthew 25, when He said that the five tardy virgins never knew Him? If you want to really **know** OWYƎⱫ, then take hold of His tears and His dreams!

Matthew 25
"Then the reign of the heavens shall be compared to ten maidens who took their lamps and went out to meet the bridegroom. ²"And five of them were wise, and five foolish. ³"Those who were foolish, having taken their lamps, took no oil with them, ⁴but the wise took oil in their containers with their lamps. ⁵"Now while the bridegroom took time, they all slumbered and slept. ⁶"And at midnight a cry was heard, 'See, the bridegroom is coming, go out to meet him!' ⁷"Then all those maidens rose up and trimmed their lamps. ⁸"And the foolish said to the wise, 'Give us of your oil, because our lamps are going out.' ⁹"But the wise answered, saying, 'No, indeed, there would not be enough for us and you. Instead, go to those who sell, and buy for yourselves.' ¹⁰"And while they went to buy, the bride-groom came, and those who were ready went in with him to the wedding feast, and the door was shut. ¹¹"And later the other maidens also came, saying, 'Master, Master, open up for us!' ¹²"But he answering, said, 'Truly, I say to you, I do not know you.' ¹³"Watch therefore, because you do not know the day nor the hour in which the Son of Adam is coming,...

Wrestle with OWYƎⱫ, Overcome with OWYƎⱫ, and Rule with OWYƎⱫ!

Tears in a Bottle

OWYƎZ agonized in the Davidic Psalms about His unprecedented afflictions, rejections, and humiliations! OWYƎZ suffered **not** for His own sins, but He suffered for ours sins and our rebellions! Yahushua's words jump off the pages and they will pierce the hearts of Israel's called out ones! It's all recorded there for Israel to discover, meditate on, and to emulate! OWYƎZ left Israel His blueprint for overcoming, while being tested by ƎYƎZ in His furnace of affliction! To be victorious, Israel **must follow Yahushua's example for overcoming! How did OWYƎZ overcome?** Look for the answers to that question as you read on!

But I, I have put my trust in You, O ƎYƎZ

Psalms 31
*In You, O ƎYƎZ, I have taken refuge; let me never be ashamed; deliver me in Your righteousness. [2]Incline Your ear to me, deliver me speedily; **be a rock of refuge to me**, a house of defense to save me. [3]For You are **my rock and my stronghold; for Your Name's sake lead me and guide me**. [4]Bring me out of the net which they have hidden for me, for You are **my stronghold**. [5]Into Your hand **I commit my spirit**; You have redeemed me, O ƎYƎZ El of truth. [6]I have hated those who observe lying vanities; but I trust in ƎYƎZ. [7]**I exult and rejoice in Your kindness, for You have seen my affliction**; You have known the distresses of my life, [8]and You have not shut me up into the hand of the enemy. You have set my feet in a large place. [9]Show me favor, O ƎYƎZ, for I am in distress; my eye, my being and my body have become old with grief! [10]For my life is consumed in sorrow, and my years in sighing; my strength fails because of my crookedness, and my bones have become old. [11]**I am a reproach among all my adversaries, but most of all among my neighbors, and a dread to my friends; those who see me outside flee from me.** [12]**I have been forgotten like someone dead from the heart; I have been like a missing vessel.** [13]**For I hear the evil report of many; fear is from all around; when they take counsel together against me, They plot to take away my life.** [14]**But I, I have put my trust in You**, O ƎYƎZ; **I have said, "You are my Elohim."** [15]**My times are in Your hand**; Deliver me from the hand of my enemies, and from those who pursue me. [16]Make Your face shine upon Your servant; **save me in Your loving-kindness**.*

Baruch ƎYƎZ!

Tears in a Bottle

You are my hiding place!

Psalms 32

For day and night Your hand was heavy upon me; my sap was turned into the droughts of summer. Selah. ⁵*<u>I acknowledged my sin to You</u>, and my crookedness I did not hide. I have said, "<u>I confess my transgressions</u> to ⳆᎩⳆᒿ," and You forgave the crookedness of my sin. Selah.* ⁶*Therefore, let every kind one <u>pray to You while You might be found</u>; even in a flood of great waters, they would not reach him.* ⁷*<u>You are my hiding place</u>; you preserve me from distress; You <u>surround me with songs of deliverance</u>. Selah.* ⁸*"<u>Let Me instruct you and teach you in the way you should go</u>; let Me counsel, my eye be on you.*

I wait for You!

Psalms 33

¹⁸*See, the eye of ⳆᎩⳆᒿ is on those fearing Him, on those waiting for His loving-kindness,* ¹⁹*To deliver their being from death, and to keep them alive during scarcity of food.* ²⁰*Our being has longed for ⳆᎩⳆᒿ; our help and our shield is He.* ²¹*For our heart does rejoice in Him, for <u>we have put our trust in His set- apart Name</u>.* ²²*Let Your loving-kindness, O ⳆᎩⳆᒿ, be upon us, even as <u>we wait for You</u>.*

Trust in ⳆᎩⳆᒿ, and do good!

Psalms 37

³*<u>Trust in ⳆᎩⳆᒿ</u>, <u>and</u> <u>do</u> <u>good</u>; Dwell in the earth, <u>and feed on steadfastness</u>.* ⁴*And <u>delight yourself in ⳆᎩⳆᒿ</u>, and <u>let Him give you the desires of your heart</u>.* ⁵*<u>Commit your way to ⳆᎩⳆᒿ</u>, and <u>trust in Him</u>, and He does it.* ⁶*And He shall bring forth your righteousness as the light, and your right-ruling as midday.* ⁷*<u>Rest in ⳆᎩⳆᒿ</u>, and <u>wait patiently</u> for Him; <u>do not fret</u> because of him, who prospers in his way, because of the man doing wicked devices.* ⁸*<u>Abstain from displeasure</u>, and <u>forsake wrath</u>; <u>do not fret, also to do evil.</u>*

Psalms 40

<u>I waited</u>, <u>waited for</u> ⳆᎩⳆᒿ; and He inclined to me, and heard my cry. ²*And He drew me out of the pit of destruction, out of the muddy clay, and He set my feet upon a rock, <u>He is establishing my steps</u>.* ³*Then <u>He put a new song in my mouth</u>; <u>praise</u> <u>to our Elohim</u>; many do see it and fear, and <u>trust in</u> ⳆᎩⳆᒿ.* ⁴*Blessed is that man who has made ⳆᎩⳆᒿ his trust, and has not turned to the proud, and those turning aside to falsehood.*

Tears in a Bottle

You put My tears into Your bottle!

Psalms 56

Show me favor, O Elohim, for man would swallow me up; fighting all day long, he oppresses me. [2]My enemies would swallow me up all day long, for many are fighting against me, O Most High. [3]In the day I am afraid, **I trust in You**. [4]In Elohim, **whose Word I praise, in Elohim I have trusted**; I do not fear; what could flesh do to me? [5]All day long they twist my words; all their thoughts are against me for evil. [6]They stir up strife, they hide, they watch my steps, as they lie in wait for my life. [7]Because of wickedness, cast them out. Put down the peoples in displeasure, O Elohim! [8]You have counted my wanderings; **You put my tears into Your bottle; are they not in Your book**? [9]My enemies turn back in the day I call; this I know, because **Elohim is for me**. [10]In Elohim, whose word I praise, in ayaz, whose word I praise, [11]in Elohim I have trusted; I do not fear; what could man do to me?

I sing aloud of Your loving-kindness!

Psalms 59

[16]And I, I sing of Your power; and in the morning <u>I sing aloud</u> of Your <u>loving-kindness</u>; for You have been my strong tower and a refuge in the day of my distress. [17]O my strength, to You I sing praises; for Elohim is <u>my strong tower</u>, <u>my Elohim of loving-kindness</u>.

Pour out your heart before ayaz!

Psalms 62

<u>My being finds rest in Elohim alone</u>; from Him is my deliverance. [2]He alone is my rock and my deliverance, my strong tower; I am not greatly shaken. [3]How long would you assail a man? You crush him, all of you, like a leaning wall, a tottering fence. [4]They plotted to topple him from his high position; they delight in lies; they bless with their mouth, but in their heart they curse. Selah. [5]My being, find rest in Elohim alone, because <u>my expectation is from Him</u>. [6]He alone is <u>my rock</u> and <u>my deliverance</u>, <u>my strong tower</u>; I am not shaken. [7]My deliverance and my esteem depend on Elohim; the rock of my strength, my refuge is in Elohim. [8]<u>Trust in Him at all times</u>, you people; <u>pour out your heart before Him</u>; Elohim is a refuge for us. Selah.

Tears in a Bottle

I remember the deeds of Yah!

Psalms 63

O Elohim, You are my El; I earnestly seek You; **my being has thirsted for You; my flesh has longed for You** in a dry and thirsty land without water. [2]Therefore I have had a vision of You in the set-apart place, to see Your power and Your esteem. [3]**Because Your loving-kindness is better than life**, **my lips do praise You**. [4]Therefore **I bless You while I live**; **in Your Name I lift up my hands**. [5]**My being is satisfied** as with marrow and fat, and **my mouth praises You with singing lips**. [6]**When I remember You on my bed**, **I meditate on You in the night watches**. [7]For You have been my help, **and in the shadow of Your wings I sing**.

My mouth is filled with Your praises!

Psalms 71

In You, O 𐤀𐤉𐤄𐤆, I have taken refuge; let me never be ashamed. [2]*In Your righteousness deliver and rescue me; incline Your ear to me, and save me.* [3]**Be to me a rock to dwell in**, *to go into continually. You have given the command to save me, for You are **my rock and my stronghold**.* [4]*Rescue me, O my Elohim, out of the hand of the wrong, out of the hand of the unrighteous and cruel.* [5]**For You are my expectation**, *master 𐤀𐤉𐤄𐤆, **my Trust from my youth**.* [6]**Upon You I have leaned from my birth; You took me out of my mother's womb. My praise is continually of You.** [7]*I have become as a wonder to many, but **You are my strong refuge**.* [8]*My mouth is filled with Your praise, Your splendor, all the day.*

Psalms 77

My voice is to Elohim, and I cry; my voice is to Elohim, and He listened to me. [2]*In the day of my distress I sought 𐤀𐤉𐤄𐤆; my hand was stretched out in the night and it did not cease, my being refused to be comforted.* [3]**I remembered Elohim**, *and groaned; I complained, and my spirit grew faint. Selah.* [4]*You ceased the watches of my eyes, I was too troubled to speak.* [5]**I have thought about the days of old**, *the years long past.* [6]**I remember my song in the night, I meditate within my heart, and my spirit searches diligently.** *Would 𐤀𐤉𐤄𐤆 reject forever, and never again be pleased?* [8]*Has His loving-kindness ceased forever, has the promise failed for all generations?* [9]*Has El forgotten to show favor? Has He shut up His compassions in displeasure? Selah.* [10]*And I said, "This is my grief: that the right hand of the Most High has changed."*

Psalms 77, cont.
11I remember the deeds of Yah, for I remember Your wonders of old.
12And I shall meditate on all Your work, and talk of Your deeds.

Bless ᄏYᄏZ for ever and ever!

Baruch ᄏYᄏZ le'olam va'ed!

**Dead Sea Scrolls
Thanksgiving Psalms**

I am satisfied for I have waited upon Your mercy!
Col 12
But, when I remembered the power of your hand together with the abundance of your mercies, I stood upright and firm and my spirit grew strong to stand against affliction. For [I] rested in Your mercies and the abundance of Your compassion.

Col 15
I give thanks to You, O ᄏYᄏZ, for **You have sustained me with Your strength, and your holy spirit You have spread over me so that I will not falter. You have strengthened me** before the wars of wickedness, and in all their devastation You have not shattered me for the sake of Your covenant. You set me up as a strong tower; as a high wall. Upon the rock, You have established my frame, and eternal foundations for my footing.

Col 15, cont.
I lean on the mult[itude of Your compassion and in the abundance of] Your mercy I await, causing the plant to blossom and a shoot to grow up; taking refuge in Your strength and [...For in] Your righteousness.

Col 17
I give an answer to those who would wipe me out, and reproof to those who would cast me down. I will condemn his verdict, but Your judgment I honor, for **I know Your truth**. **I shall choose my judgment, and with my agony I am satisfied** for **I have waited upon Your mercy**. You have put a supplication in the mouth of Your servant, and You have not rebuked my life, nor have You removed my well-being. You have not forsaken my hope, but in the face of affliction **You have restored my spirit**. **For You have established my spirit and know my deliberations**. **In my distress You have soothed me, and I delight in forgiveness**. I shall be comforted for former sin. I know that **there is hope in Your mercy**, and an expectation in the abundance of Your power. ...The contempt of my enemies has become a glorious crown for me and my stumbling, eternal strength.

Baruch ᴣᎩᴣᏃ!

Baruch ᴣᎩᴣᏃ!

I hope in Your mercy and Your forgiveness!

Col 17, cont.
For by [Your...] and Your glory, my light has shined forth, **for You have caused light from darkness to shine for me [...]You bring healing** for my wounds, for my stumbling, **wonderful strength**, an infinite space for the distress of [my] soul. **[You are] my place of refuge**, **my stronghold**, the rock of my strength and my fortress. In You I take refuge from all [...] for an eternal escape.

Tears in a Bottle

I depended upon Your compassion.

Col 19

For just as **I waited Your goodness**, so **I hope in Your mercy and Your forgiveness**. You have relieved my adversities and in my grief You have comforted me for **I depended upon Your compassion**. Blessed are You, O 𐤀𐤉𐤄𐤅, for You have done these things and You place hymns and thanksgiving in the mouth of your servant [...] and a supplication for favor as well as a suitable reply.

The rewards of Israel

Revelation 2

*"He who has an ear, let him hear what the Spirit says to the assemblies. **He who overcomes** shall by no means be harmed by the second death."'...To **him who overcomes** I shall give some of the hidden manna to eat. And I shall give him a white stone, and on the stone a renewed Name written which no one knows except him who receives it."....[26]"And **he who overcomes**, and guards My works until the end, to him I shall give authority over the nations, [27]and he shall shepherd them with a rod of iron, as the potter's vessels shall be broken to pieces, as I also have received from My Father. [28]"And I shall give him the morning star.... [5]"**He who overcomes** shall be dressed in white robes, and I shall by no means blot out his name from the Book of Life, but I shall confess his name before My Father and before His messengers.... [12]"**He who overcomes**, I shall make him a supporting post in the Dwelling Place of My Elohim, and he shall by no means go out. And I shall write on him the Name of My Elohim and the name of the city of My Elohim, the renewed Yahrushalayim, which comes down out of the heaven from My Elohim, and My renewed Name.... [21]"**To him who overcomes** I shall give to sit with Me on My throne, as **I also overcame** and sat down with My Father on His throne.*

Baruch 𐤀𐤉𐤄𐤅!

Baruch 𐤀𐤉𐤄𐤅!

Tears in a Bottle

Yahushua remembered His vows to 𐤉𐤄𐤅𐤄!

Psalms 22

My El, My El, why have You forsaken Me – Far from saving Me, far from the words of My groaning? [2]O My Elohim, I call by day, but You do not answer; And by night, but I find no rest. [3]Yet You are set-apart, enthroned on the praises of Yisra'el. [4]Our fathers trusted in You; they trusted, and You delivered them. [5]They cried to You, and were delivered; they trusted in You, and were not ashamed. [6]But I am a worm, and no man; a reproach of men, and despised by the people. [7]All those who see Me mock Me; they shoot out the lip, they shake the head, saying, [8]"He trusted in 𐤉𐤄𐤅𐤄, let Him rescue Him; let Him deliver Him, seeing He has delighted in Him!" [9]For You are the One who took Me out of the womb; causing Me to trust while on My mother's breasts. [10]I was cast upon You from birth. From My mother's belly You have been My El. [11]Do not be far from Me, for distress is near; For there is none to help. [12]Many bulls have surrounded Me; Strong ones of Bashan have encircled Me. [13]They have opened their mouths against Me, as a raging and roaring lion. [14]I have been poured out like water, and all My bones have been spread apart; My heart has become like wax; it has melted in the midst of My inward parts. [15]My strength is dried like a potsherd, and My tongue is cleaving to My jaws; and to the dust of death You are appointing Me. [16]For dogs have surrounded Me; a crowd of evil ones have encircled Me, piercing My hands and My feet; [17]I count all My bones. They look, they stare at Me. [18]They divide My garments among them, And for My raiment they cast lots. [19]But You, O 𐤉𐤄𐤅𐤄, do not be far off; O My Strength, hasten to help Me! [20]Deliver My life from the sword, My only life from the power of the dog. [21]Save Me from the mouth of the lion, and from the horns of the wild beasts! You have answered Me. [22]I make known Your Name to My brothers; in the midst of the assembly I praise You. [23]You who fear 𐤉𐤄𐤅𐤄, praise Him! All you seed of Ya'aqob, esteem Him, and fear Him, all you seed of Yisra'el! **[24]For He has not despised nor hated the affliction of the afflicted; nor has He hidden His face from Him; But when He cried to Him, He heard. [25]From You is My praise in the great assembly; I pay My vows before those who fear Him.**

Psalms 56

Show me favor, O Elohim, For man would swallow me up; Fighting all day long, he oppresses me. [2]My enemies would swallow me up all day long, for many are fighting against me, O Most High.

Tears in a Bottle

Psalms 56, cont.

³In the day I am afraid, I trust in You. ⁴In Elohim, whose Word I praise, In Elohim I have trusted; I do not fear; what could flesh do to me? ⁵All day long they twist my words; all their thoughts are against me for evil. ⁶They stir up strife, they hide, They watch my steps, as they lie in wait for my life. ⁷Because of wickedness, cast them out. Put down the peoples in displeasure, O Elohim! ⁸You have counted my wanderings; You put my tears into Your bottle; are they not in Your book? ⁹My enemies turn back in the day I call; This I know, because Elohim is for me. ¹⁰In Elohim, whose word I praise, in ⱯYⱯZ, whose Word I praise, ¹¹In Elohim I have trusted; I do not fear; what could man do to me? **¹²<u>On me, O Elohim, are Your vows</u>; I render praises to You,** *¹³For You have delivered my life from death, my feet from stumbling, that I might walk before Elohim, in the light of the living!*

Psalms 61

Hear my cry, O Elohim, listen to my prayer. ²From the end of the earth I call unto You, when my heart is faint; lead me to the rock that is higher than I. ³For You have been my refuge, a strong tower in the face of the enemy. ⁴Let me dwell in Your Tent forever, let me take refuge in the shelter of Your wings. Selah. ⁵For You, O Elohim, have heard my vows; You have given me the inheritance of those who fear Your Name. ⁶You add days to the days of the sovereign, His years as many generations. ⁷Let him dwell forever before Elohim. Prepare kindness and truth to preserve him! **⁸So I sing praise to Your Name forever, when <u>I pay my vows</u> day by day.**

Psalms 66

Shout with joy to Elohim, All the earth! ²Sing out the splendor of His Name; Make His praise esteemed. ³Say to Elohim, "How awesome are Your works! Through the greatness of Your power Your enemies pretend obedience to You. ⁴"All the earth bow to You, they sing praises to You, They praise Your Name." Selah. ⁵Come and see the works of Elohim, Awesome acts toward the sons of men. ⁶He has turned the sea into dry land, they went through the river on foot. There we rejoiced in Him, ⁷who rules by His power forever; His eyes keeping watch on the gentiles; Let the rebellious not exalt themselves. Selah. **⁸Bless our Elohim, you peoples! And sound His praise abroad, ⁹Who keeps us in life, And does not allow our feet to be moved.** *¹⁰For You, O Elohim, have proved us; You have refined us as silver is refined.*

Psalms 66, cont.

[11]*You brought us into the net; You laid affliction on our loins.* [12]*You have let men ride at our head; We went through fire and through water; But You brought us out to plenty.* [13]**I enter Your house with burnt offerings; <u>I complete my vows</u> to You,** [14]*That which my lips have uttered And my mouth spoke in my distress.* [15]*Burnt offerings of fatlings I offer to You, With the incense of rams; I offer bulls with goats. Selah.* [16]*Come, hear, all you who fear Elohim, And I relate what He has done for my being.* [17]*I called to Him with my mouth, And praise was in my tongue.* [18]*If I have seen wickedness in my heart,* **ƎΥƐZ** *would not hear.* [19]*Truly, Elohim has heard me; He has given heed to the voice of my prayer.* [20]*Blessed be Elohim, Who has not turned away my prayer, Nor His kindness from me!*

Psalms 116

I love **ƎΥƐZ**, *because He has heard my voice, my pleas.* [2]*Because He has inclined His ear to me, and I shall call throughout my days.* [3]*The cords of death were around me, and the pains of the grave came upon me; I found distress and sorrow.* [4]*Then I called upon the name of* **ƎΥƐZ**, *"O* **ƎΥƐZ**, *I pray to You, deliver my being!"* [5] **ƎΥƐZ** *shows favor and is righteous; and our Elohim is compassionate.* [6] **ƎΥƐZ** *guards the simple; I was brought low, but He saved me.* [7]*Return to your rest, O my being, For* **ƎΥƐZ** *has treated you well.* [8]*For You have delivered my being from death, My eyes from tears, My feet from falling.* [9]*I shall walk before* **ƎΥƐZ** *in the land of the living.* [10]*I have believed, for I speak; I have been greatly afflicted.* [11]*I said in my haste, "All men are liars."* [12]*What shall I return to* **ƎΥƐZ**? *All His bounties are upon me.* [13]*I lift up the cup of deliverance, and call upon the Name of* **ƎΥƐZ**. [14]**<u>I pay my vows</u> to ƎΥƐZ now in the presence of all His people.** [15]*Precious in the eyes of* **ƎΥƐZ** *is the death of* **His kind ones.** [16]*O* **ƎΥƐZ**, *I am truly Your servant, I am Your* **servant, the son of Your**

Dead Sea Scrolls
Thanksgiving Psalms XIV

I know through thy great goodness, and **with an oath I have undertaken never to sin against Thee, nor to do anything evil in Thine eyes. And thus do I bring into my community all men of my council.** I will cause each man to draw near in accordance with his understanding, and according to the greatness of his portion so will I love him. I will not honor an evil man, nor consider [the bribes of the wicked].

Thanksgiving Psalms XIV
I will [not barter] Thy truth for riches, nor one of Thy precepts for bribes. But according as [Thou drawest a man near to Thee, so will I love] him, and according as Thou movest him far from thee, so will I hate him. None of those, who have turned [from] Thy [Covenant] will I bring into the Council [of Thy truth].

Summary
When we undergo struggles and afflictions in our own lives, all of Israel must look to the example of OWY∃Z! In His sojourn on earth, OWY∃Z faced more afflictions, more rejections, more humiliations, more oppression, and more sorrow than any person, who has ever lived! So, how did OWY∃Z overcome?

ISRAEL WILL OVERCOME WITH OWY∃Z!

- **Trust** in ∃Y∃Z and His name **alone**!
- **Commit** your way to ∃Y∃Z!
- **Delight** yourself in ∃Y∃Z!
- **Remember** the Covenant of Israel with ∃Y∃Z!
- **Wait** on Yahuah's abundant mercy, compassion, loving-kindness, and forgiveness!
- **Go** to ∃Y∃Z, your strong tower, and **make** His name your place of refuge!
- **Wait patiently** on ∃Y∃Z, while continuing to **do good**!
- **Remember** Yahuah's deliverance in **the past**!
- **Remember** Yahuah's promises for **Israel's glorious future**!
- **Fulfill your vows** to ∃Y∃Z!
- **Sing** songs of praise and worship to ∃Y∃Z for His deliverance!
- **Rest** in Yahuah's promises **because you know the truth**!
- **Confess** your sins and **ask** for forgiveness in the name of ∃Y∃Z!
- **Maintain** a thankful heart and **Bless** ∃Y∃Z for all His blessings!
- **Listen** to the comfort of His Ruach HaQodesh!
- **Do not worry** about appearances, but **trust and pray** for deliverance; and **forsake** wrath!

HalleluYah! HalleluYah! HalleluYah!

Chapter 7
Good News

The Spirit of the Master ⵯⵢⵣⵍ is upon me; because ⵯⵢⵣⵍ hath anointed me to preach good tidings unto the meek; He hath sent me to bind up the brokenhearted, to proclaim liberty to the captives, and the opening of the prison to them that are bound; to proclaim the acceptable year of ⵯⵢⵣⵍ, and the day of vengeance of our Elohim; to comfort all that mourn; to appoint unto them that mourn in Zion, to give unto them beauty for ashes, the oil of joy for mourning, the garment of praise for the spirit of heaviness; that they might be called trees of righteousness, the planting of ⵯⵢⵣⵍ, that He might be glorified. **YeshaYahu** *(Isaiah)* **61**

The people, who are called Israel, will strive with OWYⵣⵍ in this world, will overcome with OWYⵣⵍ in this world, and will rule with OWYⵣⵍ in the world to come! When we are tested in Yahuah's furnace of affliction, we must follow Yahushua's example for overcoming! **Without a doubt the narrow Way of OWYⵣⵍ is very afflicted! It's hard pressed from every direction, but OWYⵣⵍ has already shown Israel how to overcome the world!** Once you make up your mind to truly follow the narrow Way of OWYⵣⵍ no matter what, **then you will be tested!** Following the narrow Way entails loving ⵯⵢⵣⵍ and OWYⵣⵍ with all your heart and obeying the Commandments of ⵯⵢⵣⵍ, not because of legalism! **You obey the Torah because you love ⵯⵢⵣⵍ and OWYⵣⵍ and want to please them! It is your chief delight to obey!** Remember, you will be tested just as every other member of Israel has been tested before you! It's not a matter of "if" your love for ⵯⵢⵣⵍ and OWYⵣⵍ will be tested, it's a matter of "**when**" you will be tested! But the overcomers of Israel should take heart and realize that **all** things **are working together** for Israel's eternal good, even when things don't add up or make any sense at all! **Do not lean on your own understanding!**

Proverbs 3:5 *Trust in ⵯⵢⵣⵍ with all thine heart; and lean **not** unto thine own understanding.*

The Righteous will suffer many afflictions in their own lives just as OWYⵣⵍ did! But at the end of the day, the Righteous will be rewarded with mind boggling gifts, just as OWYⵣⵍ was.

Tears in a Bottle

However the time available for repentance in this present age is running out because OWYƏZ will soon return to judge the wicked and unrepentant with a fiery judgment! **The hand writing is on the wall! Mene, Mene, Teqel, Upharsin!** This world has been weighed in the balance scales and has been found lacking! The reign of this present world is about to be given to another, whose days are from everlasting! The bright morning star will come riding on the clouds to judge the earth and all its inhabitants past and present! I believe that the "baby boomer generation" will see the beginning of the Day of ƏYƏZ. The generation of Israel, who are alive, when that Day begins will experience the most spectacular events in the history of mankind! There's going to be a great family reunion for all Israel! All the righteous overcomers of Israel are going to be **gathered to one place at one time to enjoy the greatest wedding celebration of all time!** All the spirits of Yahuah's overcomers, who have ever lived and died, since Yahushua's death on the Passover Tree, now rest in a place called Sheol! Sheol contains a special holding place in the underworld (under the earth) to hold the spirits of the Righteous, until the 7th Trumpet blast sounds! At that time the Righteous dead will be resurrected and will be gathered with all the rest of Israel to a fabulous celebration! All of Israel's overcomers, who lived and died, before Yahushua's death on the Passover Tree, were already resurrected **immediately after** OWYƏZ took His last breath on the Passover Tree! Those resurrected overcomers are enjoying Paradise on the heavenly Mount Zion right now as I write *Tears in a Bottle*! But they also anxiously await the sounding of the 7th Trumpet, when they **will return** with OWYƏZ and **be gathered** with all the rest of Israel to Yahushua's wedding banquet!

Matthew 27
49But the rest said, "Leave it, let us see if Eliyahu comes to save Him."
50And OWYƏZ cried out again with a loud voice, and gave up His spirit. 51And see, the veil of the Dwelling Place (on the Heavenly Mount Zion) was torn in two from top to bottom, and the earth was shaken, and the rocks were split, 52and the tombs were opened, and many bodies of the set-apart ones who had fallen asleep were raised, 53and coming out of the tombs after His resurrection, they went into the set-apart city and appeared to many.

Tears in a Bottle

When the 7th Trumpet sounds those, who are alive on the earth will be reborn into incorruptible spirit based bodies and will be gathered to the same fabulous wedding banquet!

1 Corinthians
*Behold, I shew you a mystery; we shall not all sleep, but we shall all be changed, in a moment, in the twinkling of an eye, **at the last trump: for the trumpet shall sound, and the dead shall be raised incorruptible, and we shall be changed. For this corruptible must put on <u>incorruption</u>, and this mortal must put on immortality.** So when this corruptible shall have put on incorruption, and this mortal shall have put on immortality, then shall be brought to pass the saying that is written, death is swallowed up in victory.*

Peter warned the remnant of Israel to prepare for the mocking of the scoffers at the end of the age! He also exhorted Israel to remember that a day to ᗄᎻᗄᏃ is like 1,000 years! That's a clue for the length of the Day of ᗄᎻᗄᏃ! The Day of ᗄᎻᗄᏃ will **not** be a 24 hour period of time, instead the Day of ᗄᎻᗄᏃ will be 1,000 years long!

2 Peter 3
*^{5}For they choose to have this hidden from them: that the heavens were of old, and the earth standing out of water and in the water, by the Word of Elohim, ^{6}through which the world at that time was destroyed, being flooded with water. ^{7}And the present heavens and the earth are treasured up by the same Word, being kept for <u>**FIRE**</u>, to a day of judgment and destruction of wicked men. ^{8}But, beloved ones, let not this one matter be hidden from you: that with ᗄᎻᗄᏃ <u>one day is as a thousand years</u>, and <u>a thousand years as one day</u>. ^{9} ᗄᎻᗄᏃ is not slow in regard to the promise, as some count slowness, but is patient toward us, not wishing that any should perish, but that all should come to repentance. ^{10}But the day of ᗄᎻᗄᏃ shall come as a thief in the night, in which the heavens shall pass away with a great noise, and the elements shall melt with intense heat, and the earth and the works that are in it shall be burned up. ^{11}Seeing all these are to be destroyed in this way, what kind of people ought you to be in <u>set-apart behavior</u> and <u>reverence</u>, ^{12}looking for and hastening the coming of the day of Elohim, through which the heavens shall be destroyed, being set on fire, and the elements melt with intense heat! ^{13}But according to His promise we wait for a renewed heavens and a renewed earth in which righteousness dwells.*

Tears in a Bottle

On the Day of ayaz all the overcomers of Israel, who are alive on the earth, will participate in a great worldwide Exodus from the nations back to the real Promised Land of Abraham, Isaac, and Jacob. Yes, I said Exodus, **not rapture**! The First Fruits of Israel will be gathered back to the real Promised Land just like the Prophets prophesied! The words of Yahuah's Prophets never lie because ayaz knows the end from the beginning! The prophets of ayaz wrote that this final worldwide Exodus of Israel will completely overshadow the first Exodus from Mitsrayim (mistranslated as Egypt)! The signs and wonders in the coming Exodus will be so supernatural and so spectacular that Israel will not even talk about the first Exodus! If you are very hungry for information about the future Exodus of Israel, then read my book called *Let My People Go*! You won't be sorry!

YirmeYahu 16
[14]*"Therefore see, the days are coming," declares* ayaz, *"when it is no longer said,* ayaz *lives who brought up the children of Yisra'el from the land of Mitsrayim,'* [15]*but,* ayaz *lives who brought up the children of Yisra'el from the land of the north and from all the lands where He had driven them.' For I shall bring them back into their land I gave to their fathers.*

YirmeYahu 23
[7]*"Therefore, see, the days are coming," declares* ayaz, *"when they shall say no more, 'As* ayaz *lives who brought up the children of Yisra'el out of the land of Mitsrayim,'* [8]*but, 'as* ayaz *lives who brought up and led the seed of the house of Yisra'el out of the land of the north and from all the lands where I had driven them. And they shall dwell on their own soil."*

Today the location of the real Promised Land is an enigma; it's a mystery, because it's **not located** in the place where people have been led to believe that it is located! Isn't that ironic! Doesn't that seem to be the way that it always is with the things of ayaz? Yahuah's truth always seems to be somewhere other than where popular religious thought and opinion says it is! Beware! Beware! Beware, lest Belial, satan, the liar, deceive you! Contrary to world opinion, the real Promised Land is **not** located in today's State of Israel or anywhere else in the counterfeit Land of Palestine! Palestine was established by Rome about 135 AD! The Romans put down the last Jewish revolt, which was led by Simon Bar Kochba in 135 AD!

Tears in a Bottle

The reason for the war was that Hadrian, the Roman Emperor, had misled the Jews to believe that he would rebuild Yahrushalayim and the Temple! Hadrian reneged on his promise to rebuild Yahrushalayim for the Yahudim! Instead he decided to rebuild Yahrushalayim as a Roman city and build temples to Roman gods like Jupiter! During the revolt the Romans slaughtered upwards of 500,000 Yahudim. Those not killed were exiled to other Roman provinces as slaves. Still others fled for their lives to other regions away from Roman rule. The Romans had never fought such a ferocious enemy before! During the final revolt Rome lost whole legions and were humiliated on the battle field! Never before had the Roman Legions turned and fled from any enemy. In the aftermath of the war, Hadrian decided to go one step further because of Rome's hatred of the Yahudim (Jews)! **The Romans pulled a great switch-r-rue, when they created a counterfeit Promised Land to the north of Yahrushalayim and the real Promised Land**. The Romans were called "**the boundary changers**" by the followers of OWYꝲⱫ, who hid the Dead Sea Scrolls from Roman destruction. The Romans hated the Jews! The Romans knew that they could hurt and humiliate the Jews the most by moving the location of their precious Promised Land to a counterfeit location! Well, Rome's ploy has worked to perfection from 135 AD to this very day! In 1947 the great Roman lie was revived, when today's "Holy Land" was established in Palestine! **But the time of utter darkness is almost over!** If the Promised Land is not in the State of Israel, then where is it for goodness sakes? The real Promised Land is actually located in a most surprising place! The real Promised Land is located in today's northwestern Saudi Arabia about 150-200 miles southeast of the State of Israel! **Yes, I said northwestern Saudi Arabia, not Palestine!** Isn't that a coincidence? West central Saudi Arabia is the epicenter for Islam. Muhammad made a fortune raiding caravans traveling up the incense trade route along the west coast of Saudi Arabia about 630 AD! Muhammad had visions from Belial, which were recorded! Of course, these visions spawned the birth of the Koran and the religion of Islam. The very beginnings of man (Adam and Hawwah), can be traced back to today's northwestern Arabia because that place is the true cradle of civilization! Mount Sinai is located in the land of Madyan (Median in English)! Madyan is also located in today's northwestern Saudi Arabia, **not Egypt**.

On the Day of ⳍYⳐⵑ the First Fruits of Israel will be gathered back to the real Promised Land first, where they will rebuild the ruined cities of Yahudah and Yahrushalayim itself! Today these set apart places lie in ruins in the sands of Arabia waiting for the Day of ⳍYⳐⵑ to begin! **The holy places in Palestine, which were established by Rome, are .not holy at all!** Instead, they are counterfeits and <u>snares</u> to anyone, who would place their hopes in them! The First Fruits of Israel will inhabit the real set apart places of ⳍYⳐⵑ in northwestern Saudi Arabia for 486½ years, until the cities of Yahudah and Yahrushalayim are sacked by the "Destroyer"! At the culmination of time, when the 7th Trumpet sounds, OWYⳐⵑ will return to rescue His people from Yahrushalayim! They will be surrounded by the beast and his armies! At the sound of the 7th trumpet, OWYⳐⵑ will lead Israel back to Mount Sinai, which will then be overshadowed by the heavenly Mount Zion once again as it descends from the heavens! Mount Zion will descend to her place in the wilderness above Mount Sinai, just as it was during the life of Adam! When that 7th Trumpet sounds all of Israel will be gathered to participate in the greatest wedding ceremony of all time! All the Righteous of Israel, who have waited patiently in Sheol and those still alive on the earth, will be reborn into incorruptible bodies! Ultimately Israel will have the privilege of entering into the New Yahrushalayim! And all this is just the beginning for Israel! For the Righteous overcomers of Israel there's so much to look forward to with OWYⳐⵑ!

Isaiah 64
For since the beginning of the world men have not heard, nor perceived by the ear, neither hath the eye seen, O Elohim, beside thee, what he hath prepared for him that waiteth for him.

1 Corinthians 2
9But as it has been written, "Eye has not seen, and ear has not heard, nor have entered into the heart of man what Elohim has prepared for those who love Him."

What is the Good News anyway? The Good News is that OWYⳐⵑ is returning at the sound of the 7th trumpet to bring a <u>righteous judgment to the earth</u>! No longer will the Righteous suffer the curses of sin. No longer will the Righteous be tested in Yahuah's furnace of affliction!

And no longer will the Righteous be oppressed by the wicked! The winter will be gone and the spring-time of 𐤀𐤅𐤄𐤉 will have arrived for the Righteous of Israel! 𐤏𐤅𐤄𐤉 will reward the Righteous with eternal life as elohim (mighty ones) in the family of 𐤀𐤅𐤄𐤉. The Righteous will be accepted **as better than sons and daughters** because of their love and obedience to 𐤀𐤅𐤄𐤉!

YeshaYahu 56
Thus saith 𐤀𐤅𐤄𐤉, keep ye judgment, and do justice: for my salvation is near to come, and my righteousness to be revealed. **Blessed is the man that doeth this, and the son of man that layeth hold on it; that keepeth the Sabbath from polluting it,** *and keepeth his hand from doing any evil. Neither let the son of the stranger, that hath joined himself to 𐤀𐤅𐤄𐤉, speak, saying, 𐤀𐤅𐤄𐤉 hath utterly separated me from his people: neither let the eunuch say, behold, I am a dry tree.* **For thus saith 𐤀𐤅𐤄𐤉 unto the eunuchs that keep my Sabbaths, and choose the things that please me, and take hold of my covenant; even unto them will I give in mine house and within my walls a place and a name better than of sons and of daughters:** *I will give them an everlasting name, that shall not be cut off. Also the sons of the stranger, that join themselves to 𐤀𐤅𐤄𐤉, to serve him, and to love the name of 𐤀𐤅𐤄𐤉, to be his servants, every one that keepeth the Sabbath from polluting it, and taketh hold of my covenant; even them will I bring to my holy mountain, and make them joyful in my house of prayer: their burnt offerings and their sacrifices shall be accepted upon mine altar; for mine house shall be called an house of prayer for all people. The Master 𐤀𐤅𐤄𐤉 which gathereth the outcasts of Israel saith, yet will I gather others to him, beside those that are gathered unto him.*

So then, how shall We live?
The answer to that question is contained in Psalms 119. Study this Psalms and meditate on it often! Evaluate your desires and your passions against the writer's desires and passions! When you read Psalms 119, if you see your own feelings, attitudes, desires, and passions expressed perfectly in the passage, **then you are following Yahuah's Way!** If you empathize with the writer and see yourself in His passages, then you are surely on Yahushua's narrow Way! By the way, who was speaking in Psalms 119? It was none other than Israel's Teacher of Righteousness, our Rabbi 𐤏𐤅𐤄𐤉! Finish well! Finish well! The past is past, but every new day is fresh! Finish well!

Tears in a Bottle

Finish the race that you were appointed faithfully! Trust in 𐤀𐤃𐤄𐤆 as you patiently endure, when 𐤀𐤃𐤄𐤆 tests the reins of your heart! Continue to guard the Torah of 𐤀𐤃𐤄𐤆 so that you can hit Yahuah's mark and be judged Tamiym **(complete with a Perfect Heart)**! Overcome by **remembering** Yahushua's tears! Follow Yahushua's example as you **commit** your way to 𐤀𐤃𐤄𐤆! **Trust** in the abundance of Yahuah's mercies and His loving-kindness! Then **rest** in the wonderful name of 𐤀𐤃𐤄𐤆!

Psalms 119

Blessed are the perfect in the way, who walk in the teaching of ᚠᚥᚨᚦ!
[2]Blessed are those who observe His witnesses, who seek Him with all the heart! [3]Yea, they shall do no unrighteousness; they shall walk in His ways. [4]You have commanded us to guard Your orders diligently. [5]Oh, that my ways were established to guard Your laws! [6]Then I would not be ashamed, when I look into all Your commands. [7]I thank You with uprightness of heart, when I learn the right-rulings of Your righteousness. [8]I guard Your laws; oh, do not leave me entirely! [9]How would a young man cleanse his path? To guard it according to Your word! [10]I have sought You with all my heart; let me not stray from Your commands! [11]I have treasured up Your word in my heart, that I might not sin against You. [12]Blessed are You, O ᚠᚥᚨᚦ! Teach me Your laws. [13]With my lips I have recounted all the right-rulings of Your mouth. [14]I have rejoiced in the way of Your witnesses, as over all riches. [15]I meditate on Your orders, and regard Your ways. [16]I delight myself in Your laws; I do not forget Your word. [17]Do good to Your servant, let me live and I guard Your word. [18]Open my eyes, that I might see wonders from Your Torah. [19]I am a sojourner in the earth; do not hide Your commands from me. [20]My being is crushed with longing for Your right-rulings at all times. [21]You rebuked the proud, cursed ones, who are straying from Your commands. [22]Remove from me reproach and scorn, for I have observed Your witnesses. [23]Though princes sat, speaking against me, Your servant meditates on Your laws. [24]Your witnesses also are my delight, my counselors. [25]My being has been clinging to the dust; revive me according to Your word. [26]I have recounted my ways and You answered me; teach me Your laws. [27]Make me understand the way of Your orders; that I might meditate on Your wonders. [28]My being has wept from grief; strengthen me according to Your word. [29]Remove from me the way of falsehood, and favor me with Your Torah. [30]I have chosen the way of truth; Your right-rulings I have held level.

Psalms 119, cont

[31]I have clung to Your witnesses; O יהוה, do not put me to shame! [32]I run the way of Your commands, for You enlarge my heart. [33]Teach me, O יהוה, the way of Your laws, and I observe it to the end. [34]Make me understand, that I might observe Your Torah, and guard it with all my heart. [35]Make me walk in the path of Your commands, for I have delighted in it. [36]Incline my heart to Your witnesses, and not to own gain. [37]Turn away my eyes from looking at falsehood, and revive me in Your way. [38]Establish Your word to Your servant, which leads to the fear of You. [39]Turn away my reproach which I dread for Your right-rulings are good. [40]See, I have longed for Your orders; revive me in Your righteousness. [41]And let Your kindnesses come to me, O יהוה; Your deliverance, according to Your word, [42]So that I answer my reprover, for I have trusted in Your word. [43]And do not take away from my mouth the word of truth entirely, for I have waited for Your right-rulings; [44]that I might guard Your Torah continually, forever and ever; [45]that I might walk in a broad place, for I have sought Your orders; [46]that I might speak of Your witnesses before sovereigns, and not be ashamed; [47]That I might delight myself in Your commands, which I have loved; [48]That I might lift up my hands to Your commands, which I have loved; while I meditate on Your laws. [49]Remember the word to Your servant, On which You have caused me to wait. [50]This is my comfort in my affliction, for Your word has given me life. [51]The proud have utterly scorned me, I did not turn aside from Your Torah. [52]I remembered Your right-rulings of old, O יהוה, and I comfort myself. [53]Rage has seized me because of the wrong who forsake Your Torah. [54]Your laws have been my songs in the place of my sojournings. [55]I have remembered Your Name in the night, O יהוה, and I guard Your Torah. [56]This has become mine, because I have observed Your orders. [57]You are my portion, O יהוה; I have promised to guard Your words. [58]I have sought Your face with all my heart; show me favor according to Your word. [59]I have thought upon my ways, and turned my feet to Your witnesses. [60]I have hurried, and did not delay to guard Your commands. [61]The cords of the wrong have surrounded me, Your Torah I have not forgotten. [62]At midnight I rise to give thanks to You, for Your righteous right-rulings. [63]I am a companion of all who fear You, and of those guarding Your orders. [64]O יהוה, Your kindness has filled the earth; teach me Your laws. [65]You have done good to Your servant, O יהוה, according to Your word. [66]Teach me good sense and knowledge, for I have trusted in Your commands.

Tears in a Bottle

Psalms 119, cont
[67]Before I was afflicted I myself was going astray, but now I have guarded Your word. [68]You are good, and do good; teach me Your laws. [69]The proud have forged a lie against me, with all my heart I observe Your orders. [70]Their heart has become like fat, without feeling; I have delighted in Your Torah. [71]It was good for me that I was afflicted, that I might learn Your laws. [72]The Torah of Your mouth is better to me than thousands of gold and silver pieces. [73]Your hands have made me and formed me; Make me understand, that I might learn Your commands. [74]Those who fear You see me and rejoice, for I have waited for Your Word. [75]I know, O 𐤉𐤄𐤅𐤄, that Your right-rulings are righteous, and in trustworthiness You have afflicted me. [76]Please let Your kindness be for my comfort, according to Your word to Your servant. [77]Let Your compassions come to me, that I might live, for Your Torah is my delight. [78]Let the proud be put to shame, for with lies they perverted me; but I study Your orders. [79]Let those who fear You turn to me, and those who know Your witnesses. [80]**_Let my heart be perfect in Your laws, so that I am not put to shame._** [81]For Your deliverance my being has pined away, for I have waited for Your word. [82]My eyes have pined away for Your word, Saying, "When would it comfort me?" [83]For I have become like a wineskin in the smoke, Your laws I have not forgotten. [84]How many are the days of Your servant? When do You execute right-ruling on those who persecute me? [85]The proud have dug pits for me, which is not according to Your Torah. [86]All Your commands are trustworthy; they have persecuted me with lies; Help me! [87]They almost made an end of me on earth, but I, I did not forsake Your orders. [88]Revive me according to Your kindness, that I might guard the witness of Your mouth. [89]Forever, O 𐤉𐤄𐤅𐤄, Your word stands firm in the heavens. [90]Your trustworthiness is to all generations; You established the earth, and it stands. [91]According to Your right-rulings They have stood to this day, for all are Your servants. [92]If Your Torah had not been my delight, I would have perished in my affliction. [93]Let me never forget Your orders, For by them You have given me life. [94]I am Yours, save me; for I have sought Your orders. [95]The wrong have waited for me to destroy me; I understand Your witnesses. [96]I have seen an end of all perfection; Your command is exceedingly broad. [97]O how I love Your Torah! It is my study all day long. [98]Your commands make me wiser than my enemies; for it is ever before me. [99]I have more understanding than all my teachers, for Your witnesses are my study.

Psalms 119, cont.

[100]I understand more than the aged, for I have observed Your orders. [101]I have restrained my feet from every evil way, that I might guard Your word. [102]I have not turned aside from Your right-rulings, for You Yourself have taught me. [103]How sweet to my taste has Your word been, more than honey to my mouth! [104]From Your orders I get understanding; therefore I have hated every false way. [105]Your word is a lamp to my feet and a light to my path. [106]I have sworn, and I confirm, to guard Your righteous right-rulings. [107]I have been afflicted very much; O יהוה, revive me according to Your word. [108]Please accept the voluntary offerings of my mouth, O יהוה, and teach me Your right-rulings. [109]My life is in my hand continually, and Your Torah I have not forgotten. [110]The wrong have laid a snare for me, but I have not strayed from Your orders. [111]Your witnesses are my inheritance forever, for they are the joy of my heart. [112]I have inclined my heart to do Your laws forever, to the end. [113]I have hated doubting thoughts, but I have loved Your Torah. [114]You are my hiding place and my shield; I have waited for Your word. [115]Turn away from me, you evil-doers, for I observe the commands of my Elohim! [116]Support me according to Your word, that I might live; and put me not to shame because of my expectation. [117]Sustain me, that I might be saved, and always look to Your laws. [118]You have made light of all those who stray from Your laws, for falsehood is their deceit. [119]You have made to cease all the wrong of the earth, like dross; therefore I have loved Your witnesses. [120]My flesh has trembled for fear of You, and I am in awe of Your right-rulings. [121]I have done right-ruling and righteousness; leave me not to my oppressors. [122]Guarantee Your servant's well-being; let not the proud oppress me. [123]My eyes have pined away for Your deliverance, and for the word of Your righteousness. [124]Do with Your servant according to Your kindness, and teach me Your laws. [125]I am Your servant – make me understand, that I might know Your witnesses. [126]It is time for יהוה to act! For they have broken Your Torah. [127]Therefore I have loved Your commands more than gold, even fine gold! [128]Therefore all Your orders I count as right; I have hated every false way. [129]Your witnesses are wonders; so my being observes them. [130]The opening up of Your words gives light, giving understanding to the simple. [131]I have opened my mouth and panted, for I have longed for Your commands.

Psalms 119, cont.

[132]Turn to me and show me favor, according to Your right-ruling, toward those, who love Your Name. [133]Establish my footsteps by Your word, and let no wickedness have rule over me. [134]Redeem me from the oppression of man, that I might guard Your orders. [135]Make Your face shine upon Your servant, and teach me Your laws. [136]Streams of water have run down from my eyes, because they did not guard Your Torah. [137]Righteous are You, O 𐤀𐤙𐤀𐤆, and Your right-rulings are straight. [138]You have commanded Your witnesses in righteousness and truth, exceedingly. [139]My ardor has consumed me, for my adversaries have forgotten Your words. [140]Your word is tried, exceedingly; and Your servant has loved it. [141]I am small and despised; I have not forgotten Your orders. [142]Your righteousness is righteousness forever, and Your Torah is truth. [143]Distress and anguish have found me; Your commands are my delight. [144]The righteousness of Your witnesses is forever; make me understand, that I might live. [145]I have called with all my heart; answer me, O 𐤀𐤙𐤀𐤆! I observe Your laws. [146]I have called upon You; save me, that I might guard Your witnesses. [147]I rise before dawn, and cry for help; I have waited for Your word. [148]My eyes have gone before the night watches, to study Your word. [149]Hear my voice according to Your kindness; O 𐤀𐤙𐤀𐤆, revive me according to Your right-ruling. [150]Those who pursue mischief have drawn near; they have been far from Your Torah. [151]You are near, O 𐤀𐤙𐤀𐤆, and all Your commands are truth. [152]Of old I have known Your witnesses, that You have founded them forever. [153]See my affliction and deliver me, for I have not forgotten Your Torah. [154]Plead my cause and redeem me; revive me according to Your word. [155]Deliverance is far from the wrong ones, for they have not sought Your laws. [156]Your compassions are many, O 𐤀𐤙𐤀𐤆; revive me according to Your right-rulings. [157]My persecutors and adversaries are many; I have not turned aside from Your witnesses. [158]I saw traitors and was grieved, because they did not guard Your word. [159]See how I have loved Your orders, 𐤀𐤙𐤀𐤆, revive me according to Your kindness. [160]The sum of Your word is truth, and all Your righteous right-rulings are forever. [161]Rulers have persecuted me without a cause, but at Your word my heart stood in awe. [162]I rejoice at Your word as one who finds great treasure. [163]I have hated falsehood and loathe it, Your Torah I have loved. [164]I have praised You seven times a day, because of Your righteous right-rulings. [165]Great peace have those loving Your Torah, and for them there is no stumbling-block.

Psalms 119, cont.
[166] ⲀⲨⲀⱫ, I have waited for Your deliverance, and I have done Your commands. [167]My being has guarded Your witnesses, and I love them exceedingly. [168]I have guarded Your orders and Your witnesses, for all my ways are before You. [169]My cry comes before You, O ⲀⲨⲀⱫ; make me understand according to Your word. [170]Let my prayer come before You; deliver me according to Your word. [171]My lips pour forth praise, for You teach me Your laws. [172]My tongue sings of Your word, for all Your commands are righteousness. [173]Your hand is a help to me, for I have chosen Your orders. [174]I have longed for Your deliverance, O ⲀⲨⲀⱫ, and Your Torah is my delight. [175]My being lives, and it praises You; and Your right-rulings help me. [176]I have strayed like a lost sheep; seek Your servant, for **I have not forgotten Your commands**.

The End!

Dear OWYⱯⱫ,

Thank You so much for trusting me of all people to retell your Story for the Children of Israel in my days!

Todah ⲀⲨⲀⱫ! Todah ⲀⲨⲀⱫ!

Todah ⲀⲨⲀⱫ!

The Burning Bush

²And the Messenger of 𐤉𐤄𐤅𐤄 appeared to him in a flame of fire from the midst of a bush. and he looked and saw the bush burning with fire, but the bush was not consumed. Exodus 3

Now here is a mystery! Remember the encounter that Moses had with the Messenger of 𐤉𐤄𐤅𐤄 (OWY𐤄Z) in the "Burning Bush" at Mount Sinai! Moses was told that he must go back to Mitzrayim (not Egypt) and speak to the Pharaoh of Mitzrayim and the children of Israel! 𐤉𐤄𐤅𐤄 had heard the cry of Israel and had seen the cruelty of their task masters! 𐤉𐤄𐤅𐤄 remembered His promises to Abraham, Isaac, and Jacob and was ready to act because of His great name! Moses was instructed to deliver Yahuah's messages of deliverance to the powerful Pharaoh! Moses asks, "What if the Pharaoh won't believe me?" This is what the Messenger of 𐤉𐤄𐤅𐤄 told Moses to do!

Exodus 4
*And Mosheh answered and said, "And if they do not believe me, nor listen to my voice, and say, '𐤉𐤄𐤅𐤄 has not appeared to you?' " ²And 𐤉𐤄𐤅𐤄 said to him, "What is that in your hand?" And he said, **"A rod."** ³And He said, **"Throw it on the ground."** So he threw it on the ground, and **it became a serpent**. And Mosheh fled from it. ⁴And 𐤉𐤄𐤅𐤄 said to Mosheh, **"Reach out your hand and take it by the tail"** – so he reached out his hand and caught it, and **it became a rod in his hand** –⁵so that they believe that 𐤉𐤄𐤅𐤄 Elohim of their fathers, the Elohim of Abraham, the Elohim of Yitshaq, and the Elohim of Ya'aqob, has appeared to you." ⁶And 𐤉𐤄𐤅𐤄 said to him again, **"Now put your hand in your bosom."** And he put his hand in his bosom, and when he took it out, and **see, his hand was leprous**, like snow. ⁷And He said, **"Put your hand in your bosom again."** So he put his hand in his bosom again, and drew it out of his bosom, and see, **it was restored like his other flesh**. ⁸"And it shall be, if they do not believe you, nor listen to the voice of the first sign, they shall believe the voice of the latter sign. "And it shall be, if they do not believe even these two signs, or listen to your voice, that you shall take water from the river and pour it on the dry land. And the water which you take from the river shall become blood on the dry land."*

Why did 𐤉𐤄𐤅𐤄 choose these signs for Moses to demonstrate, before the Pharaoh? Selah, think about this very carefully!

Tears in a Bottle

Near the end of the age Israel will experience a fabulous worldwide Exodus from the nations. The coming Exodus will be epic in proportion, when compared to the first Exodus! It will be completely supernatural and will pale the signs and wonders done during the first Exodus! Can you imagine that? OWYƼZ will be Israel's deliverer in Israel's coming worldwide Exodus. He will lead Israel back to the **real** Promised Land! Remember Yahuah's promise to Moses!

Deuteronomy 18 (Moses)
I will raise them up a Prophet from among their brethren, like unto thee, and will put my words in his mouth; and He shall speak unto them all that I shall command him. And it shall come to pass, that whosoever will not hearken unto my words which he shall speak in my name, I will require it of him.

First OWYƼZ was Clean, then Unclean, then Clean again!

The signs that Moses was instructed to perform in front of the Pharaoh were <u>not</u> random signs! Moses was instructed to take His rod and to cast it down to the ground. When he did, the rod of ƼYƼZ turned into a devouring serpent. Then Moses was instructed to pick the rod up by its tail! When Moses picked the rod up, the serpent turned back into the rod of ƼYƼZ. This sign has direct relevance to Yahushua's sojourn on earth as Israel's Passover Lamb! OWYƼZ is the rod of ƼYƼZ! It was Yahushua's own choice to completely humble Himself in Yahuah's crucible of affliction and to lay down His Life for the lost sheep of Israel! OWYƼZ willingly humbled and humiliated Himself because OWYƼZ <u>had</u> <u>a</u> <u>dream</u> <u>for</u> <u>Israel</u>! OWYƼZ became cursed as symbolized by the serpent, not because of His own sin, **but because of the sins and rebellions of others, which include my sins and rebellions!** But just as it was Yahushua's decision to cast down His own life, OWYƼZ took up His life again by the power of ƼYƼZ! The pattern of the first sign was **EXALTED**; then **CURSED**; then **EXALTED** again! And so it was with OWYƼZ! Think about it, Selah!

John 10
[14]"I am the good shepherd. And I know mine, and mine know me, [15]even as the Father knows Me, and I know the Father. And **I <u>lay down</u> my life for the sheep**. [16]"And other sheep I have which are not of this fold – I have to bring them as well, and they shall hear my voice, and there shall be one flock, one shepherd.

Tears in a Bottle

John 10, cont.
[17] *"Because of this the Father loves me, because I lay down my life, in order to receive it again.* [18] *"No one takes it from me, but I lay it down of myself. I have authority to lay it down, and I have authority to receive it again.* This command I have received from my Father."

For the second sign Moses was instructed to reach his hand inside His bosom, and then to withdraw it. When Moses withdrew his hand it was leprous and unclean! Then Moses was instructed to put his hand into his bosom again and then to withdraw it. When Moses withdrew his hand this time, his hand was clean! Again this sign has direct relevance to OWYƷZ! The pattern for the second sign was **CLEAN**, then **UNCLEAN** with Leprosy, then **CLEAN** again! And so it was with OWYƷZ during His first sojourn on the earth! But what about the third sign? Water was turned to blood! Remember when the Roman soldier pierced the side of OWYƷZ on the Passover Tree! What came out? Water, then blood spilled from the body of OWYƷZ! Isn't it interesting how the three of the signs given to Moses were all manifested in the life of OWYƷZ, when He came as Israel's Passover Lamb? But what will happen in the future? Will we see the signs of Moses again, when OWYƷZ returns to judge the earth's inhabitants? Examine the seven bowl judgments of Revelation for yourself. On the day of ƎYƷZ every single wicked soul will be resurrected and will face the wrath of ƎYƷZ! Every single wicked soul from every generation will be resurrected and gathered together for torture and destruction on the Day of ƎYƷZ! During Yahushua's agonies on earth, He spoke curses on the wicked, who were trying to kill Him! **Every** **single** **one** of Yahushua's curses on the wicked and unrepentant will come to pass on the Day of ƎYƷZ! Woe be it to them! Woe be it to them! Woe be it to them!

Psalms 35
O ƎYƷZ, strive with those who strive with me; **fight against those who fight against me.** [2] Take hold of shield and armor, and rise for my help. [3] And draw out spear and lance, to meet those who pursue me. Say to my life, "I am your deliverance." [4] **Let those be ashamed and blush who seek my life;** let those be turned back and abashed, **who plot evil to me.** [5] Let them be as chaff before the wind with a messenger of ƎYƷZ driving on. [6] Let their way be dark and slippery, with a messenger of ƎYƷZ pursuing them.

Tears in a Bottle

Psalms 35, cont.
[7]*For without cause they hid their net for me; without cause they dug a pit for my life.* [8]*Let ruin come upon him unawares, and let his net that he hid catch himself; let him fall in it, into ruin.* [9]*But let my own being exult in* 𐤉𐤄𐤅𐤄*; let it rejoice in His deliverance.* [10]*Let all my bones say, "*𐤉𐤄𐤅𐤄*, who is like You, delivering the poor from one stronger than he, and the poor and the needy from him who robs him?"* [11]*Ruthless witnesses rise up; they ask me that which I knew not.* [12]*They reward me evil for good, bereaving my life.* [13]*But I, when they were sick, I put on sackcloth; I humbled my being with fastings; and my prayer would return to my own bosom.* [14]*I walked about as though he were my friend or brother; I bowed down mourning, as one mourning for a mother.* [15]*But they rejoiced at my stumbling and gathered together; the smiters gathered against me, and I did not know it; they tore in pieces without ceasing,* [16]*With unclean ones, mockers at feasts, gnashing at me with their teeth.* [17]𐤉𐤄𐤅𐤄*, how long would You look on? Rescue my being from their destructions, my only life from the lions.* [18]*I give You thanks in the great assembly; I praise You among a mighty people.* [19]**Let not my lying enemies rejoice over me; or those who hate me without cause wink their eyes.** [20]*For they do not speak peace, but they devise words of deceit against the peaceable ones of the land.* [21]*And they open their mouth wide against me, they said, "**Aha, Aha**! Our eyes have seen it."* [22]*This You have seen, O* 𐤉𐤄𐤅𐤄*; do not be silent. O* 𐤉𐤄𐤅𐤄*, do not be far from me.* [23]*Stir up Yourself and awake to my right-ruling – to my cause, my Elohim and my Master.* [24]*Rule me rightly, O* 𐤉𐤄𐤅𐤄 *my Elohim, according to Your righteousness; and let them not rejoice over me.* [25]*Let them not say in their hearts, "**Aha, our desire!**" Let them not say, "We have swallowed him up."*

Psalms 69
[19]**You Yourself know my reproach, and my shame and my confusion; my adversaries are all before You.** [20]**Reproach has broken my heart and I am sick; I looked for sympathy, but there was none; and for comforters, but I found none.** [21]*And they gave me gall for my food, and for my thirst they gave me vinegar to drink.* [22]*Let their table before them become a snare, and a trap to those at ease.* [23]**Let their eyes be darkened, so as not to see; and make their loins shake continually.**

Psalms 69, cont.

^{24}Pour out Your wrath upon them, and let Your burning displeasure overtake them. **^{25}Let their encampments be deserted; let no one dwell in their tents. ^{26}For they persecute him whom You have smitten, and talk about the pain of those You have wounded.** ^{27}Add crookedness to their crookedness, and let them not enter into Your righteousness. **^{28}Let them be blotted out of the book of the living, and not be written with the righteous.** ^{29}But _I am poor and in pain_; let Your deliverance, O

Psalms 40

^{14}Let those who seek to destroy my life be ashamed and abashed altogether; let those who are desiring my evil be driven back and put to shame. ^{15}Let those who say to me, "Aha, Aha!" be appalled at their own shame. ^{16}Let all those who seek You Rejoice and be glad in You; let those who love Your deliverance always say, "𐤉𐤄𐤅𐤄 be exalted!"

Psalms 70

O Elohim, deliver me! Hasten to my help, O 𐤉𐤄𐤅𐤄! **^{2}Let those who seek my life be ashamed and abashed, let those who are desiring my evil be turned back and humiliated. ^{3}Let those who say, "_Aha, Aha_!"**

Psalms 140

^{4}Guard me, O 𐤉𐤄𐤅𐤄, from the hands of the wrong; guard me from a man of violence, who have **_schemed to trip up my steps_**. ^{5}The proud have hidden a trap for me, and cords; they have spread a net by the wayside; they have set snares for me. Selah. ^{6}I said to 𐤉𐤄𐤅𐤄, "You are my El; Hear the voice of my prayers, O 𐤉𐤄𐤅𐤄. ^{7}"O Master 𐤉𐤄𐤅𐤄, my saving strength, You have screened my head in the day of battle. ^{8}"Do not grant the desires of the wrong, O 𐤉𐤄𐤅𐤄; do not promote his scheme. Selah. ^{9}"Those who surround me lift up their head; the trouble of their lips cover them; **^{10}Let burning coals fall on them; let them be made to fall into the fire, Into deep pits, let them not rise again.** ^{11}"Let not a slanderer be established in the earth; let evil hunt the man of violence speedily." ^{12}I have known that 𐤉𐤄𐤅𐤄 maintains the cause of the afflicted, the right-ruling of the poor. ^{13}Only, let the righteous give thanks to Your name, let the straight ones dwell in Your presence.

Tears in a Bottle

No idle word came out of Yahushua's mouth! 𐤉𐤄𐤅𐤄 counted all of Yahushua's tears as He captured them in His bottle! Every blessing for Israel and every curse for the wicked spoken by 𐤏𐤅𐤄𐤅𐤉𐤄 will occur on the Day of 𐤉𐤄𐤅𐤄! __All the wicked from every generation will be plagued with leprosy for their rebellion against__ 𐤉𐤄𐤅𐤄! **(Revelation Bowl of Wrath #1)** What goes around comes around, right? Turn-about is fair play! These wicked souls hated 𐤉𐤄𐤅𐤄 and they hated His only begotten son, 𐤏𐤅𐤄𐤅𐤉𐤄! The wicked mocked 𐤏𐤅𐤄𐤅𐤉𐤄! They spit on Him! They laughed at 𐤏𐤅𐤄𐤅𐤉𐤄! They joked unmercifully about Yahushua's suffering and agony! They harassed and plotted to kill Him at every turn! They even sang songs about the leper scholar! This was 𐤏𐤅𐤄𐤅𐤉𐤄 your Messiah, the lover of your soul that I'm talking about! The wicked deserve everything they will get! I have no sympathy for them at all! 𐤏𐤅𐤄𐤅𐤉𐤄 __will turn all their water to blood__ (Bowls of Wrath 2/3)! Then 𐤏𐤅𐤄𐤅𐤉𐤄 will __turn the heat of the sun way up to scorch men with the heat__! **(Bowl of wrath #4)** Then 𐤏𐤅𐤄𐤅𐤉𐤄 will bring complete darkness to their land! They will all have leprosy! There won't be any water for them to drink! The sun will become much, much hotter, and the wicked and unrepentant will experience **total darkness**! **(Bowl #5)** When the **Revelation Bowl of Wrath #6 is poured out on the earth, the river Phratt in Saudi Arabia will be dried up** to allow the wicked to assemble for their destruction in the winepress of Yahuah's fury at the valley of Yahushofet (Valley of Yahu's Judgment)! Then 𐤏𐤅𐤄𐤅𐤉𐤄 will crush their wicked armies in the winepress of His fury at the valley of Yahushofet **with fiery hail stones weighing 100 pounds each! (Bowl #7)** Their will be no remnant or survivor for the wicked and unrepentant! **Woe be it to them! Woe be it to them! Woe be it to them!** When you are in Yahuah's furnace being tested in His crucible, take heart! Remember the Burning Bush! **The bush __burned__, but it was __not__ consumed! This is the way it is with the called out ones of Israel!**

Psalms 37

Do not fret because of evil-doers, do not be envious of the workers of unrighteousness. [2]For they soon wither like grass, and fade like green plants. [3]Trust in 𐤉𐤄𐤅𐤄, and do good; dwell in the earth, and feed on steadfastness. [4]And delight yourself in 𐤉𐤄𐤅𐤄, and let Him give you the desires of your heart. [5]Commit your way to 𐤉𐤄𐤅𐤄, and trust in Him, and He does it. [6]And He shall bring forth your righteousness as the light, and your right-ruling as midday.

Psalms 37, cont.
[7]Rest in יהוה, and wait patiently for Him; do not fret because of him who prospers in his way, because of the man doing wicked devices. [8]Abstain from displeasure, and forsake wrath; do not fret, also to do evil. [9]For evil-doers are cut off; but those who wait on יהוה, they shall inherit the earth. [10]Yet a little while and the wrong is no more; and you shall look on his place, but it is not. [11]But the meek ones shall inherit the earth, and delight themselves in plenty of peace. [12]The wrong plots against the righteous, and gnashes his teeth at him. [13]יהוה laughs at him, for He sees that his day is coming. [14]The wrong have drawn the sword and have bent their bow, to cause the poor and needy to fall, to slay those who walk straightly. [15]Their sword does enter into their own heart, and their bows are broken. [16]Better is the little of the righteous one, than the riches of many wrongdoers. [17]For the arms of the wrongdoers are broken, but יהוה sustains the righteous. [18]יהוה knows the days of the perfect, and their inheritance is forever. [19]They are not ashamed in a time of evil, and in the days of scarcity of food they are satisfied. [20]But the wrongdoers shall perish; and the enemies of יהוה, like the splendor of the meadows they vanish, like smoke they vanish away. [21]The wrongdoer is borrowing and does not repay, but the righteous one shows favor and gives. [22]For His blessed ones inherit the earth, but those cursed by Him are cut off. [23]The steps of a man are ordered by יהוה, and He delights in his way. [24]Though he falls, he is not cast down, for יהוה is supporting his hand. [25]I have been young, and now I am old; yet I have not seen the righteous forsaken, or his seed begging bread. [26]All day long he is showing favor and lending; and his seed is for a blessing. [27]Turn away from evil, and do good; and dwell forever. [28]For יהוה loves right-ruling, and does not forsake His kind ones; they shall be guarded forever, but the seed of the wrongdoers is cut off. [29]The righteous shall inherit the earth, and dwell in it forever. [30]The mouth of the righteous speaks wisdom, and his tongue talks of right-ruling [31]The Torah of his Elohim is in his heart; his steps do not slide. [32]The wrong one is watching for the righteous, and is seeking to slay him. [33]יהוה does not leave him in his hand, or let him be declared wrong when he is judged. [34]Wait on יהוה and guard His way, and He shall exalt you to inherit the earth – when the wrongdoers are cut off, you shall see it.

Psalms 37, cont.
[35]I have seen the wrongdoer in great power, and spreading himself like a native green tree. [36]Yet he passed away, and see, he was not; and I sought him, but he was not found. [37]Watch the perfect, and observe the straight; for the latter end of each is peace. [38]But the transgressors shall be destroyed together; the latter end of the wrong shall be cut off. [39]But the deliverance of the righteous is from ᴤYᴤZ, their strength in time of distress. [40]And ᴤYᴤZ does help them and deliver them; He delivers them from the wrongdoers and saves them, because they took refuge in Him.

Israel will experience struggles in the fire of Yahuah's furnace, but they will **not** be consumed! When Israel comes out of Yahuah's furnace of testing, **they will not even smell like smoke**! HalleluYah! HalleluYah! HalleluYah! Many are the afflictions of the Righteous, but ᴤYᴤZ carries the Righteous through them all! Yahuah's overcomers, Israel, will **not** be destroyed even though the circumstances may **appear** completely hopeless and your spirit may be depressed! But take heart and remember the tears of OWYᴤZ! Remember OWYᴤZ was tested in every way just as we are and so much more! **Follow Yahushua's principals for overcoming this world!** And remember Israel will **wrestle** with OWYᴤZ in this world, Israel will **overcome** with OWYᴤZ in this world, and Israel will be **exalted** with OWYᴤZ in the world to come!

Bless ᴤYᴤZ!

Baruch ᴤYᴤZ!

Baruch ᴤYᴤZ!

Baruch ᴤYᴤZ!

OWYᴚꓒ and the Dead Sea Scrolls

Since 1947, I believe that more books and essays have been written on the subject of the Dead Sea Scrolls than any other spiritual subject! The Scrolls are a priceless treasure for the people called Israel, but they have been shrouded in a veil of mystery, since their discovery in 1945 by a young Bedouin goat herder named Muhammad edh-Dhib. I find it interesting that ᴚYᴚꓒ used a lowly goat to lead mankind to rediscover this lost written treasure! In the summer of 1945 Muhammad was trailing a goat, which was lost from his flock, when he discovered a cave in the cliffs bordering the northwestern shore of the Dead Sea. Since 1947 many renowned scholars have labored intensely for over 60 years trying to piece together the secrets of the more than 800 documents collectively known as the Dead Sea Scrolls. Wonderful evidence about OWYᴚꓒ exists in the Dead Sea Scrolls, but scholars and laymen alike have been blinded to the truth about the Scroll's contents! What should be impossible to miss has been rationalized away because of erroneous assertions made by spiritually blinded men! Most of the so-called experts cannot see the truth because they are spiritually blinded! The blind leading the blind seems to be a consistent pattern in this crazy world, doesn't it? The Scrolls have been shrouded in a maze of confusion, which was created early on by Father de Vaux's poor management of resources and his rule of secrecy! But, how can so many of the world's greatest scholars misinterpret what should jump off the pages right before their very eyes? Selah, go figure that out! Since 1947, measures were taken by the powers controlling the Scrolls to tightly control texts released to the media and to the public! Many documents were not released to the public in a timely manner! And there is no way to know what precious treasures have been withheld altogether from Yahuah's hungry sheep! The biggest reasons for the confusion surrounding the Scrolls center around two erroneous assertions made by powerful men! These two assumptions have been promoted as the truth by the powers controlling the Scrolls! The first erroneous assumption is that the Dead Sea Scrolls were composed in whole or in part at Qumran and then stored in caves by a group of people called the Essenes! The second misleading assumption is that all the Dead Sea Scrolls were written and hidden before the time of Yahushua! Most scholars date the Scrolls to the period 200 BC to 70 AD, which by the way does overlap the life of OWYᴚꓒ!

Tears in a Bottle

Carbon dating of the linen wrap covering the Scrolls dates back to the time period 200 BC to well beyond 70 AD! I smell a rat! Don't you? Since 1947 more than 800 documents have been found in eleven different Caves. Many of these documents are very old fragments of books from the Scriptures! Others like *The Book of Enoch* are copies of ancient non canonized documents dating back to the days of Israel's earliest Patriarchs! *The Book of Enoch* is an extremely important book because it provides a good foundation of understanding for events that occurred, before the Flood! *The Book of Enoch* contains very important information about the events before the Flood and at the end of the age! For hundreds of years *The Book of Enoch* has been suppressed and lost. But I'll go on record and say flatly that *The Book of Enoch* should have been canonized all along!

The Scrolls found in the Qumran Caves embody a wide spectrum of very important spiritual documents from many different time periods, **including the time period** of OWYႬL! Did you get that? **I said that some documents in the Scrolls are documents written during the time period of OWYႬL and afterwards by the followers of OWYႬL**! It's quite likely that OWYႬL wrote some of the documents Himself! The Thanksgiving Psalms could have been written directly by OWYႬL or someone else may have written them for Him in earlier times or someone living during Yahushua's lifetime! Remember David was used as Yahuah's instrument to write the many Davidic Psalms of the Scriptures! In the Davidic Psalms OWYႬL speaks from the first person perspective! Over the years political, religious, and financial powers have perpetuated incorrect notions about the Scrolls! Some scholars insist that the Scrolls predate the birth of the Messiah, OWYႬL, by 50 to 100 years! Incorrect assumptions put forward by so called scholars, have caused OWYႬL to be rejected from consideration as the rightful owner of the title, "**The Teacher of Righteousness**" and "**The Interpreter of the Torah**"! The wicked High Priest Caiaphas is "**The Wicked Priest**", who relentlessly conspired to kill OWYႬL! How hard is that to figure out? How sad that is, but you know powerful people have agendas and those agendas don't include ႬYႬL! If you are really interested in the Dead Sea Scrolls, then get Norman Golb's book, *Who Wrote the Dead Sea Scrolls*. But my favorite books containing actual English translations of the Scrolls are *The Dead Sea Scrolls* and *The Complete Dead Sea Scrolls in English* by Geza Vermes.

Tears in a Bottle

Who hid the Scrolls?

The Essenes **did** **not** write or hide the Dead Sea Scrolls unless they followed OWYAZ! Yahushua's followers fled from Yahrushalayim and the cities of Yahudah in the wake of Roman destruction in 70 AD! The first century assembly that followed OWYAZ of Natzareth, the Teacher of Righteousness, hid the Scrolls to keep them from being destroyed!

Acts 2

Then Kepha said unto them, repent, and be baptized every one of you in the name of OWYAZ the Messiah for the forgiveness of sins, and ye shall receive the gift of the Holy Spirit. For the promise is unto you, and to your children, and to all that are afar off, even as many as AYAZ our Elohim shall call. And with many other words did he testify and exhort, saying, save yourselves from this untoward generation. Then they that gladly received his word were baptized: and the same day there were added unto them about three thousand souls. And they continued steadfastly in the apostles' doctrine and fellowship, and in breaking of bread, and in prayers. And fear came upon every soul: and many wonders and signs were done by the apostles. And all that believed were together, and had all things common; and sold their possessions and goods, and parted them to all men, as every man had need. And they, continuing daily with one accord in the temple, and breaking bread from house to house, did eat their meat with gladness and singleness of heart, praising AYAZ, and having favor with all the people. And AYAZ added to the assembly daily such as should be saved.

Acts 4

*And as they spake unto the people, the priests, and the captain of the temple, and the Sadducees, came upon them, being grieved that they taught the people, and preached through OWYAZ the resurrection from the dead. And they laid hands on them, and put them in hold unto the next day: for it was now eventide. Howbeit many of them which heard the word believed; and the number of the men was about five thousand. And it came to pass on the morrow, that their rulers, and elders, and scribes, And Annas the high priest, and Caiaphas **(the Wicked Priest)**, and John, and Alexander, and as many as were of the kindred of the high priest, were gathered together at Yahrushalayim. And when they had set them in the midst, they asked, by what power, or by what name, have ye done this?*

Acts 4, cont.
Then Kepha, filled with the Holy Spirit **(Ruach HaQodesh),** said unto them, Ye rulers of the people, and elders of Israel, if we this day be examined of the good deed done to the impotent man, by what means he is made whole; be it known unto you all, and to all the people of Israel, that by the name of OWY37 the Messiah of Natzareth, whom ye crucified, whom 3Y37 raised from the dead, even by him doth this man stand here before you whole. **This is the stone which was set at nought of you builders, which is become the head of the corner. Neither is there salvation in any other: for there is none other name under heaven given among men, whereby we must be saved.** Now when they saw the boldness of Kepha and John, and perceived that they were unlearned and ignorant men, they marveled; and they took knowledge of them, that they had been with OWY37. And beholding the man which was healed standing with them, they could say nothing against it. But when they had commanded them to go aside out of the council, they conferred among themselves, saying, what shall we do to these men? For that indeed a notable miracle hath been done by them is manifest to all them that dwell in Yahrushalayim; and we cannot deny it. But that it spread no further among the people, let us straitly threaten them, that they speak henceforth to no man in this name. And they called them, and commanded them not to speak at all nor teach in the name of OWY37. But Kepha and John answered and said unto them, whether it be right in the sight of Elohim to hearken unto you more than unto 3Y37, judge ye. For we cannot but speak the things, which we have seen and heard. So when they had further threatened them, they let them go, finding nothing how they might punish them, because of the people: for all men glorified 3Y37 for that which was done. For the man was above forty years old on whom this miracle of healing was shewed. And being let go, they went to their own company, and reported all that the chief priests and elders had said unto them. And when they heard that, they lifted up their voice to 3Y37 with one accord, and said, 3Y37, thou art Elohim, which hast made heaven, and earth, and the sea, and all that in them is: Who by the mouth of thy servant David hast said, Why did the heathen rage, and the people imagine vain things? The kings of the earth stood up, and the rulers were gathered together against 3Y37, and against his Messiah.

Acts 4, cont.

For of a truth against thy holy child OWY⅄Ⅎ, whom thou hast anointed, both Herod, and Pontius Pilate, with the Gentiles, and the people of Israel, were gathered together, for to do whatsoever thy hand and thy counsel determined before to be done. And now, ⅄Y⅄Ⴎ, behold their threatenings: and grant unto thy servants, that with all boldness they may speak thy word, by stretching forth thine hand to heal; and that signs and wonders may be done by the name of thy holy child OWY⅄Ⅎ. And when they had prayed, the place was shaken where they were assembled together; and they were all filled with the Holy Spirit (Ruach HaQodesh), and they spake the word of ⅄Y⅄Ⴎ with boldness.

And <u>the multitude of them</u> that believed were of <u>one heart and of one soul</u>: neither said any of them that ought of the things which he possessed was his own; but <u>they had all things common</u>. And with great power gave the apostles witness of the resurrection of the Master OWY⅄Ⅎ: and great favor was upon them all. Neither was there any among them that lacked: for as many as were possessors of lands or houses sold them, and brought the prices of the things that were sold, and laid them down at the apostles' feet: and distribution was made unto every man according as he had need.

The **followers** of OWY⅄Ⅎ of Natzareth, the anointed one of ⅄Y⅄Ⴎ, actually hid the Scrolls in the caves of Qumran in order to save them from Roman destruction! The threat of destruction first occurred in 70 AD during the first Jewish revolt against Rome, and it reoccurred again in 135 AD during the second Jewish revolt lead by Simon Bar Kochba! The Temple and most of the city of Yahrushalayim were destroyed in 70 AD by the Roman general Titus, but in 135 AD the destruction by Hadrain's ruthless armies was complete and equally devastating! Yahrushalayim was literally plowed under by the Romans! Hundreds of other Jewish cities and strongholds were obliterated by the Romans during the final rebellion! In the aftermath of the Bar Kochba revolt, the Romans earned the title of "the boundary changers", which is often alluded to in the Dead Sea Scrolls! The Romans under the direction of Hadrian reinvented a counterfeit Yahrushalayim, which is called Jerusalem today, but was originally called Aelia Capitalina to the north of the real Promised Land! The Romans moved the boundaries of the Promised Land north to a place, which they called the Land of Palestine, a further insult to Israel! Of course that Roman lie is still alive and well today in the modern State of Israel!

Tears in a Bottle

Why does a relative nobody like me understand these secrets, while the world's scholars and experts remain boggled up in their never ending debates? Here's the answer!

1 Corinthians 1
Because the foolishness of ⴰⵢⴰⵣ is wiser than men; and the weakness of ⴰⵢⴰⵣ is stronger than men. For ye see your calling, brethren, how that not many wise men after the flesh, not many mighty, not many noble, are called: *But ⴰⵢⴰⵣ <u>hath chosen the foolish things of the world to confound the wise</u>; and ⴰⵢⴰⵣ hath chosen the weak things of the world to confound the things which are mighty; And base things of the world, and things which are despised, hath ⴰⵢⴰⵣ chosen, yea, and things which are not, to bring to nought things that are: That no flesh should glory in his presence.* But of him are ye in the Messiah Oⴸⵢⴰⵣ, who of ⴰⵢⴰⵣ is made unto us wisdom, and righteousness, and sanctification, and redemption: That, according as it is written, He that glorieth, let him glory in ⴰⵢⴰⵣ.

1 Corinthians 2
That your faith should not stand in the wisdom of men, but in the power of ⴰⵢⴰⵣ. Howbeit we speak wisdom among them that are perfect: yet not the wisdom of this world, nor of the princes of this world, that come to nought: But we speak the wisdom of ⴰⵢⴰⵣ in a mystery, even the hidden wisdom, which ⴰⵢⴰⵣ ordained before the world unto our glory: Which none of the princes of this world knew: for had they known it, they would not have crucified the King of glory. But as it is written, eye hath not seen, nor ear heard, neither have entered into the heart of man, the things which Elohim hath prepared for them that love him. *But ⴰⵢⴰⵣ hath revealed them unto us by his Spirit: for the Spirit searcheth all things, yea, the deep things of ⴰⵢⴰⵣ.* For what man knoweth the things of a man, save the spirit of man which is in him? Even so the things of Elohim knoweth no man, but the Spirit of Elohim. Now we have received, not the spirit of the world, but the spirit which is of Elohim; that we might know the things that are freely given to us of ⴰⵢⴰⵣ. *Which things also we speak, not in the words which man's wisdom teacheth, but which the Holy Spirit teacheth; comparing spiritual things with spiritual. But the natural man receiveth not the things of the Spirit of ⴰⵢⴰⵣ: for they are foolishness unto him: neither can he know them, because <u>they are spiritually discerned</u>.*

Tears in a Bottle

OWYƎZ, the Teacher of Righteousness

The only teacher of Righteousness, who has ever lived, is **OWYƎZ**! The followers of **OWYƎZ** referred to Him repeatedly as their teacher! The Hebrew word for teacher is Rabbi! As you will see, when you examine the Scriptures below, there are many witnesses that **OWYƎZ** was widely known as the Teacher of Righteousness! The followers of **OWYƎZ** as well as His enemies acknowledged **OWYƎZ** as a great Rabbi! **OWYƎZ** amazed men all over Israel with His unparalleled wisdom and understanding of the Torah, and remember it started, when **OWYƎZ** was only twelve years old!

Matthew 9:11 *And when the Pharisees saw it, they said unto his disciples, why eateth your Rabbi with publicans and sinners?*

Matthew 12:38 *Then certain of the scribes and of the Pharisees answered, saying, Rabbi, we would see a sign from thee.*

Matthew 17:24 *And when they were come to Capernaum, they that received tribute money came to Kepha, and said, doth not your Rabbi pay tribute?*

Matthew 19:16 *And, behold, one came and said unto him, good Rabbi, what good thing shall I do, that I may have eternal life?*

Matthew 22:16 *And they sent out unto him their disciples with the Herodians, saying, Rabbi, we know that thou art true, and teachest the way of Elohim in truth, neither carest Thou for any man: for thou regardest not the person of men.*

Matthew 22:24 *Saying, Rabbi, Moses said, if a man die, having no children, his brother shall marry his wife, and raise up seed unto his brother.*

Matthew 22:36 *Rabbi, which is the great commandment in the law?*

Matthew 23:7 *And greetings in the markets, and to be called of men, Rabbi, Rabbi.*

Matthew 23:8 *But be not ye called Rabbi: for one is your Rabbi, even the Messiah; and all ye are brethren.*

Matthew 26:18 *And He said, go into the city to such a man, and say unto him, the Rabbi saith, My time is at hand; I will keep the Passover at thy house with my disciples.*

Matthew 26:25 *Then Judas, which betrayed Him, answered and said, Rabbi, is it I? He said unto him, Thou hast said.*

OWY3Z, the Teacher of Righteousness

Matthew 26:49 *And forthwith he came to* **OWY3Z**, *and said, Greetings, Rabbi; and kissed him.*

Mark 4:38 *And He was in the hinder part of the ship, asleep on a pillow: and they awake him, and say unto him, Rabbi, carest thou not*

Mark 9:5 *And Kepha answered and said to* **OWY3Z**, *Rabbi, it is good for us to be here: and let us make three tabernacles; one for thee, and one for Moses, and one for EliYah.*

Mark 9:38 *And John answered Him, saying, Rabbi, we saw one casting out devils in thy name, and he followeth not us: and we forbad him, because he followeth not us.*

Mark 10:17 *And when He was gone forth into the way, there came one running, and kneeled to Him, and asked him, Good Rabbi, what shall I do that I may inherit eternal life?*

Mark 10:20 *And he answered and said unto him, Rabbi, all these have I observed from my youth.*

Mark 10:35 *And James and John, the sons of Zebedee, come unto him, saying, Rabbi, we would that thou shouldest do for us whatsoever we shall desire.*

Mark 11:3 *And if any man say unto you, why do ye this? Say ye that the Rabbi hath need of him; and straightway he will send him hither.*

Mark 11:21 *And Kepha calling to remembrance saith unto him, Rabbi, behold, the fig tree which thou cursedst is withered away.*

Mark 12:14 *And when they were come, they say unto him, Rabbi, we know that thou art true, and carest for no man: for thou regardest not the person of men, but teachest the way of Elohim in truth: Is it lawful to give tribute to Caesar, or not?*

Mark 12:19 *Rabbi, Moses wrote unto us, if a man's brother die, and leave his wife behind him, and leave no children, that his brother should take his wife, and raise up seed unto his brother.*

Mark 12:32 *And the scribe said unto him, well, Rabbi, thou hast said the truth: for there is one Elohim; and there is none other but he:*

Mark 13:1 *And as He went out of the temple, one of his disciples saith unto him, Rabbi, see what manner of stones and what buildings are here!*

OWY꒣꒒, the Teacher of Righteousness

Mark 14:14 *And wheresoever he shall go in, say ye to the good man of the house, the Rabbi saith, where is the guest chamber, where I shall eat the Passover with my disciples?*

Mark 14:45 *And as soon as he was come, he goeth straightway to him, and saith, Rabbi, Rabbi; and kissed him.*

Luke 5:12 *And it came to pass, when He was in a certain city, behold a man full of leprosy: who seeing OWY꒣꒒ fell on his face, and besought him, saying, Rabbi, if thou wilt, thou canst make me clean.*

Luke 6:46 *And why call ye Me, Rabbi, Rabbi, and do not the things which I say?*

Luke 9:54 *And when his disciples James and John saw this, they said, Rabbi, wilt thou that we command fire to come down from heaven, and consume them, even as EliYah did?*

Luke 9:57 *And it came to pass, that, as they went in the way, a certain man said unto him, Rabbi, I will follow thee whithersoever thou goest.*

Luke 9:59 *And He said unto another, Follow me. But he said, Rabbi, suffer me first to go and bury my father.*

Luke 9:61 *And another also said, Rabbi, I will follow thee; but let me first go bid them farewell, which are at home at my house.*

Luke 10:17 *And the seventy returned again with joy, saying, Rabbi, even the devils are subject unto us through thy name.*

Luke 10:40 *But Martha was cumbered about much serving, and came to him, and said, Rabbi, dost thou not care that my sister hath left me to serve alone? Bid her therefore that she help me.*

Luke 11:1 *And it came to pass, that, as He was praying in a certain place, when He ceased, one of his disciples said unto him, Rabbi, teach us to pray, as John also taught his disciples.*

Luke 12:41 *Then Kepha said unto him, Rabbi, speakest thou this parable unto us, or even to all?*

Luke 13:23 *Then said one unto him, Rabbi, are there few that be saved?*

Luke 17:37 *And they answered and said unto him, Where, Rabbi? And He said unto them, wheresoever the body is, thither will the eagles be gathered together.*

Luke 18:41 *Saying, What wilt thou that I shall do unto thee? And he said, Rabbi, that I may receive my sight.*

Tears in a Bottle

OWYᴧZ, the Teacher of Righteousness

Luke 19:8 And Zakkai stood, and said unto OWYᴧZ; Behold, Rabbi, the half of my goods I give to the poor; and if I have taken any thing from any man by false accusation, I restore him fourfold.

Luke 19:31 And if any man ask you, why do ye loose him? Thus shall ye say unto him, because the Rabbi hath need of him.

Luke 19:34 And they said, the Rabbi hath need of him.

Luke 22:33 And he said unto him, Rabbi, I am ready to go with thee, both into prison, and to death.

Luke 22:38 And they said, Rabbi, behold, here are two swords. And he said unto them, it is enough.

Luke 22:49 When they which were about him saw what would follow, they said unto him, Rabbi, shall we smite with the sword?

Luke 23:42 And he said unto OWYᴧZ, Rabbi, remember me when thou comest into thy kingdom.

John 1:38 Then OWYᴧZ turned, and saw them following, and saith unto them, what seek ye? They said unto him, Rabbi, where dwellest thou?

John 1:49 Nathanael answered and saith unto him, Rabbi, thou art the Son of ᴧYᴧZ; thou art the King of Israel.

There are many more examples that I did not include, but you get the picture, don't you? After reading all those verses, there should be no doubt in anyone's mind that OWYᴧZ was well known as **the Teacher of Righteousness** by all His followers and by His enemies!

Prophet, Priest, Teacher, Servant, and King

OWYᴧZ is the mighty one of Yahu (EliYahu) spoken of by the prophet, Malachi! The disciples had been taught from their childhood that EliYahu would come, before the Messiah returned to deliver Israel and to judge the earth! That is all perfectly true! However, the lost sheep of Israel did not recognize EliYahu, when they **SAW** Him! EliYahu, the mighty one of ᴧYᴧZ, did come and His name was OWYᴧZ! OWYᴧZ is the mighty one of ᴧYᴧZ! He first came as Yahuah's prophet, Yahuah's messenger, Yahuah's teacher, Yahuah's servant, and Yahuah's sacrificial Lamb! On the Day of ᴧYᴧZ, OWYᴧZ will return once again as Yahuah's Judge, Yahuah's Champion, and Yahuah's King!

OWYƏZ is the Teacher of Righteousness! OWYƏZ is Yahuah's high priest in the order of Malkitsedeq! Malkitsedeq was the priest of the most high, who offered bread and wine to ƏYƏZ at Salem, when He met Abraham, after Abraham's rescue of Lot! OWYƏZ offered His own bread and wine, **not for His own sins, but for the sins of others**! OWYƏZ offered His own blood and his own flesh for our sins and rebellions! OWYƏZ is the anointed prophet, EliYahu, the mighty one of Yahu, and the suffering servant of YeshaYahu (Isaiah) 53! For it was YeshaYahu, who said, "Who will believe our report?" And finally OWYƏZ is the King of Israel from the line of King David, who will bring justice to the whole earth, when He sets up His Kingdom at the end of the age!

EliYahu

Malachi 4
But unto you that fear my name shall the Sun of righteousness (OWYƏZ) arise with healing in his wings; and ye shall go forth, and grow up as calves of the stall. And ye shall tread down the wicked; for they shall be ashes under the soles of your feet in the day that I shall do this, saith ƏYƏZ of hosts. Remember ye the law of Moses my servant, which I commanded unto him in Horeb for all Israel, with the statutes and judgments. Behold, I will send you EliYah ((OWYƏZ) the prophet before the coming of the great and dreadful day of ƏYƏZ: And he shall turn the heart of the fathers to the children, and the heart of the children to their fathers, lest I come and smite the earth with a curse.

John 1
*And this is the record of John, when the Jews sent priests and Levites from Jerusalem to ask him, who art thou? And he confessed, and denied not; but confessed, I am not the Messiah. And they asked him, What then? Art thou EliYah? And he saith, **I am not**. Art thou that prophet? **And he answered, No.** Then said they unto him, who art thou? That we may give an answer to them that sent us. What sayest thou of thyself? He said, I am the voice of one crying in the wilderness, make straight the way of ƏYƏZ, as said the prophet Isaiah.*

Matthew 17
And His disciples asked him, saying, why then say the scribes that EliYah must first come? And OWYƏZ answered and said unto them, EliYah truly shall first come, and restore all things.

Matthew 17, cont.
But I say unto you, that EliYah is come already, and they knew him not, but have done unto him whatsoever they listed. Likewise shall also the Son of man suffer of them. Then the disciples understood that He spake unto them of John the Baptist. **(The disciples believed that** OWYƷZ **was speaking of John the Baptist, but He was actually speaking of Himself!)**

Malkitsedeq

Hebrew 5
So also the Messiah glorified not himself to be made an high priest; but He that said unto him, thou art my Son, today have I begotten thee. As He saith also in another place, Thou art a priest for ever after the order of Malkitsedeq. Who in the days of his flesh, when He had offered up prayers and supplications with strong crying and tears unto Him that was able to save Him from death, and was heard in that He feared; Though He were a Son, yet learned He obedience by the things which He suffered; and being made perfect, He became the author of eternal salvation unto all them that obey Him; called of ƷYƷZ *an high priest after the order of Malkitsedeq.*

Hebrew 7
[21]For they indeed became priests without an oath, but He became Priest with an oath by Him who said to Him, "ƷYƷZ has sworn and shall not regret, 'You are a priest forever according to the order of Malkitsedeq.' [22]By as much as this OWYƷZ has become a guarantor of a better covenant. [23]And indeed, those that became priests were many because they were prevented by death from continuing, [24]but He, because He remains forever, has an unchangeable priesthood. [25]Therefore He is also able to save completely those who draw near to Elohim through Him, ever living to make intercession for them. [26]For it was fitting that we should have such a High Priest – kind, innocent, undefiled, having been separated from sinners, and exalted above the heavens, [27]who does not need, as those high priests, to offer up slaughter offerings day by day, first for His own sins and then for those of the people, for this He did once for all when He offered up Himself. [28]For the Torah appoints as high priests men who have weakness, but the word of the oath which came after the Torah, appoints the Son having been perfected forever.

Tears in a Bottle

Dead Sea Scrolls 4Q541, Servant Poem

He (OWY੧Z) will atone for all the children of His generation and He will be sent to all the children of His [pe]ople. His word is like a word of heaven and His teaching is in accordance with the will of ੧Y੧Z! His eternal sun will shine, and His light will be kindled in all the corners of the earth, and it will shine in the darkness. Then the darkness will pass away [fro]m the earth, and thick darkness from the dry land.

Psalms 2

*Why do the heathen rage, and the people imagine a vain thing? The kings of the earth set themselves, and the rulers take counsel together, against ੧Y੧Z, and against **His anointed**,(OWY੧Z) saying, let us break their bands asunder, and cast away their cords from us. He that sitteth in the heavens shall laugh: ੧Y੧Z shall have them in derision. Then shall He speak unto them in His wrath, and vex them in his sore displeasure. Yet have I set my king upon my holy hill of Zion. I will declare the decree: ੧Y੧Z hath said unto Me, **Thou art my Son; this day have I begotten thee. Ask of me, and I shall give thee the heathen for thine inheritance, and the uttermost parts of the earth for thy possession.** Thou shalt break them with a rod of iron; thou shalt dash them in pieces like a potter's vessel. Be wise now therefore, O ye kings: be instructed, ye judges of the earth. **Serve ੧Y੧Z with fear, and rejoice with trembling. Kiss the Son, lest He be angry, and ye perish from the way, when His wrath is kindled but a little. Blessed are all they that put their trust in Him.***

Psalms 45

*My heart is bubbling up a good matter: I speak of the things which I have made touching the king: my tongue is the pen of a ready writer. Thou art fairer than the children of men: favor is poured into thy lips: therefore Elohim hath blessed thee for ever. Gird thy sword upon thy thigh, O most mighty, with thy glory and thy majesty. And in thy majesty ride prosperously because of truth and meekness and righteousness; and thy right hand shall teach thee terrible things. Thine arrows are sharp in the heart of the king's enemies; whereby the people fall under thee. **Thy throne, O Elohim, is for ever and ever: the scepter of thy kingdom is a right scepter. Thou lovest righteousness, and hatest wickedness: therefore Elohim, thy Elohim, hath anointed thee with the oil of gladness above thy fellows**. All thy garments smell of myrrh, and aloes, and cassia, out of the ivory palaces, whereby they have made thee glad.*

Our Story

[28]And we know that all matters work together for good to those who love Elohim, to those who are called according to His purpose. Romans 8:28

I grew up in a middle class southern household in Augusta, Georgia. My parents were both Christians, who faithfully attended the same Baptist church for almost 50 years! My parents were very good to my brother and me! They gave us both what we needed to be successful in this life! My mother is retired now, but she was an outstanding school teacher, who was old school all the way! She still helps many people, especially older people, who are home bound or just experiencing hard times! My father was a real "Field and Stream" man! Hunting and fishing were his great passions! He helped me over the years numerous times, when I really needed it! When my brother and I were both young, my parents ensured that we both attended Sunday school and church every Sunday, unless we were out of town! At nine years old I attended our church's annual two week revival! It was at that time that I first felt the Ruach HaQodesh convicting my heart! Of course at that time I didn't know anything about Hebrew or the Ruach HaQodesh, but I did know that I was feeling extreme pressure, while sitting on my pew! The visiting evangelist, who was preaching that revival, was Adrian Rogers! Adrian Rodgers became a very well known Baptist preacher! He was broadcast nationally on television for many years! Ironically, the sermon that night was titled "Armageddon"! That sermon was the first teaching on the end times that I had ever heard! Whenever a visiting preacher came to the church for a revival, it was a tradition for the children to get the autograph of the visiting preacher in their Bibles, after the service! The children would line up for the visiting preacher to sign his autograph and write a Bible verse inside their Bibles! When Adrian Rodgers signed my Bible, he wrote Romans 8:28!

Romans 8: 28
[28]And we know that all matters work together for good to those who love Elohim, to those who are called according to His purpose.

Little did I know back then, but that verse was to become my life's verse! It has been a constant source of hope and comfort to me from that day forward!

Tears in a Bottle

As a young adult, I was very naive about people and the ways of this world! As many people do, I married the first girl, who came along! As a young person I was good by the standards of society! I taught Sunday school in the Youth Department for several years, but never could figure out why those kids weren't more excited about the Scriptures and their promises! After three years of marriage, my wife decided that I wasn't what she wanted! She left along with our six month old daughter, Leslie! That was heart breaking for me! When my wife left, I was crushed! I did the only thing that I knew to do! I searched the Scriptures for answers! It was then that I read the Scriptures from cover to cover for the very first time! During that first crisis and every crisis, since then, I have survived by consuming the Scriptures! Now the Scriptures are my food and my water everyday! I study and meditate on the Scriptures everyday for my very own personal survival! All my dreams and desires hang on Yahuah's promises! Yahuah's Word has sustained me all my life! The immediate aftermath of that marriage was an extremely difficult time for me and my family! I give 𐤀𐤉𐤀𐤆 all the credit for carrying me through the grieving process, even though I didn't even know Yahuah's name back then! After a while, I married an unusually strong and virtuous young woman named Vicki Lynn Barnes! Vicki and I have been married for 23 years! We are alike in a lot of ways! We are both extremely family oriented! We love each other and we love our children! We even love the same movies! Vicki is a very rare commodity in today's world because in the end she follows her husband no matter what! That characteristic has proven to be very important, when we finally decided to follow Yahuah's ways and not the ways of this world, no matter what! Vicki nurtures the whole family each and everyday! I know that 𐤀𐤉𐤀𐤆 hand picked Vicki for us because of her strength, toughness, and determination! 𐤀𐤉𐤀𐤆 knew that our family would need a woman like that in order to fulfill our destiny! Vicki and I have three children! Kasey is twenty years old and she's our oldest daughter! Kasey epitomizes the daughter that I always saw in my dreams! She is beautiful inside and out! She's very creative, very insightful, and very kind to everyone no matter what their abilities or disabilities! Kasey is a stellar student, an obedient daughter, and she has always been extremely virtuous! Christian is fifteen and he's my first born son! Christian was named in honor of the promise that I made to 𐤀𐤉𐤀𐤆, when I asked 𐤀𐤉𐤀𐤆 for a son!

Tears in a Bottle

Of course, when I prayed Hannah's prayer, I didn't even know, who Hannah was, or the name of the mighty one that I was created to serve! Christian is a wonderful son in everyway! He was created, after my own image, but only better! Christian has a very quiet nature and he's very practical! He has the wisdom of a wise old man, but he has a warrior's spirit, which manifests itself on the baseball field! Christian never quits on the baseball field and will never quit on 𐤀𐤉𐤀𐤆, no matter what! Our youngest son Chad is fourteen! Chad is the most amicable of all our children! He has a very kind and compassionate heart! Chad has great compassion for people, who are suffering with diseases, especially children! Chad loves his family very much and is often brought to tears, when saying his goodbyes! Chad is very tough and gets the most out of every minute of every day! He absolutely loves the outdoors! Chad never goes anywhere without making new friends and he's always willing to help with a project! Tools, clothes, and shoes, especially tennis shoes and boots, are Chad's favorite material things! The makeup of our family would not be complete without a discussion about Leslie! Leslie is twenty-five and my daughter from my first marriage! Leslie and I were both born on November 15th in the same hospital twenty five years apart! Leslie is a very kind and very gentle person on the one hand, but she has no trouble taking charge in critical situations! I guess that's why Leslie is such a good nurse in the Heart Intensive Care unit at the local hospital! Leslie is a great story teller, she has boundless enthusiasm, and she is always ready for an adventure!
Our lives made a quantum change, when Chad contracted Juvenile Diabetes, when he was two years old! Chad almost died, when the doctors misdiagnosed his disease twice before finally recognizing the problem weeks later! Since that time Chad and the whole family have been profoundly affected by Chad's continuous struggle with that disease! A few years later Christian was diagnosed with Perthes Disease, which causes the femur bones to disintegrate in the hip sockets! Last year Kasey was diagnosed with a thyroid and a heart condition, which has caused Kasey to experience dizziness, numbness, and weight loss! We are fighting that battle right now! In January of 2006 I was working in New Mexico and living alone in an apartment, far away from my family and my familiar Georgia surroundings! A few months earlier I was laid off from a job that I had held for 24 years because of company downsizing!

Tears in a Bottle

While I was working in New Mexico, my father was very, very sick at home in Augusta, Georgia! My life seemed to be overflowing with problems and I was sixteen hundred miles from home! But I remembered Romans 8:28 and I meditated on it often, while there! Just in time ⴰⲎⴰⵣ brought me back home to work at the same place where I had worked for the previous 24 years! The day, after I got home, my father went back into the hospital for the last time! He died a few days later with my family and my mother present in the room! I closed his eyes for the last time! I started this book, while I was alone in New Mexico! Looking back ⴰⲎⴰⵣ must have known that I needed solitude and undivided time to start *Let My People Go*!

In a very strange way the pressures of Chad's Diabetes, Christian's Perthes Disease, Kasey's condition, and all the other struggles have been the catalysts that have provoked me to zealously search the Scriptures for answers and hope! I understand a little bit about how Jacob must have felt, when He was questioned by the Pharaoh of Mitsrayim, after Jacob was reunited with Joseph!

Genesis 47
[7]And Yoseph brought in his father Ya'aqob and set him before Pharaoh. And Ya'aqob blessed Pharaoh. [8]And Pharaoh said to Ya'aqob, "How old are you?" [9]And Ya'aqob said to Pharaoh, The days of the years of my sojournings are one hundred and thirty years. <u>Few and evil have been the days of the years of my life</u>, and they have not reached the days of the years of the life of my fathers in the days of their sojournings."

I started searching for answers about my sons' diseases first, but I found out so much more! I did <u>not</u> understand it back then, but my real destiny hangs on the knowledge that I have learned about ⴰⲎⴰⵣ! The insight and understanding that Yahuah's Ruach HaQodesh has given me has far surpassed my wildest imaginations! Yahuah's Scriptures are becoming more and more clear to me everyday! Yahuah's Ruach HaQodesh teaches me the right Way to go and has given me a love for the people of Israel! About eight years ago this love surfaced and led me to investigate the Hebrew roots of the Scriptures! For several years I financially supported *The Wings of Eagles*, which is an organization that airlifts Jews out of Russia to the State of Israel! I also supported several settlements in the State of Israel as well as other ministries there as well!

Tears in a Bottle

At that time we were going to a full gospel church, which stressed, "Healing is for today!" There were many very sincere Christians at that church, who we still love, but there were many red flags that we saw as time went by! The pastor held a <u>strange</u>, almost mesmerizing, hold over the sheep! The pastor was very charismatic and a great communicator! She used the power of words to lead a large group of people in a certain direction, which she always determined, of course! That church was a "feel good kind of place" with a lot of dancing and celebration! However, over time I discovered that deception, secrecy, and control reigned supreme there!

Revelation 2

[20]"But I hold against you that you allow that woman Izebel, who calls herself a prophetess, to teach and lead My servants astray to commit whoring and to eat food offered to idols. [21]"And I gave her time to repent of her whoring, and she did not repent. [22]"See, I am throwing her into a sickbed, and those who commit adultery with her into great affliction, <u>unless they repent of their works</u>.

After a while I no longer felt comfortable in that church! I left and started attending a very small Messianic congregation! I was at a crossroad and Vicki had to determine, if she would follow my lead! I did <u>not</u> pressure Vicki at all, but Kasey and Vicki studied on their own and convinced themselves that <u>I was indeed telling the truth</u>! When they determined to follow me, they didn't realize it then, but they were about to go further and further against the grain of popular opinion as we traveled on our spiritual journey! It was at that time that Vicki and the rest of the family stopped celebrating Christmas, Easter, and all the rest of the contaminated Christian holidays! Vicki, who had been a huge Christmas person all her life, took both of our artificial trees, her wooden reindeer, all her lights, and all the other trappings and put them at the road for the garbage collector! Wow, I was so proud of Vicki and Kasey that day! That had to be ﾁﾕﾁﾆ, who caused such a huge change in Vicki! Like I said, Vicki's one in a million! Initially, I felt like that Messianic congregation <u>must</u> be where we belonged, but as I kept studying and learning, I knew that something was still missing!
I knew that somehow there was so much more! While that Messianic congregation did celebrate the Shabbat and the Festivals, they didn't use the real names of ﾁﾕﾁﾆ and OWﾕﾁﾆ at all! That puzzled me greatly!

I noticed that Messianic Judaism had its own gaggle of man-made traditions, which many times over-shadowed the real Commandments of **𐤀𐤉𐤄𐤆**! All the people in our congregation observed Yahuah's Festivals, but had no problem with celebrating the pagan Festivals of Christmas, Easter, etc. too! That inconsistency vexed me! At that time I read *The Two Babylons, Fossilized Customs,* and *Come Out of Her My People* for the very first time! I was reading everything that I could get my hands on about the origins of paganism and the history of the Christian church! At that time I came to the shocking realization of what apostasy was all about and how sinister its deception is! The pieces were coming together for me and my eyes were wide open! I was upset, terrified, and broken hearted because of the depth of the deception that has snared so many millions of well meaning people over so many generations! I'm sorry, but I have stop right here just a minute and be painfully honest! If you are a preacher serving as a shepherd over any congregation of sheep and you've been exposed to the truth about Christmas, Easter, and the set apart names of **𐤀𐤉𐤄𐤆** and **O𐤅𐤉𐤄𐤆**, then <u>you</u> <u>should</u> <u>be</u> <u>very</u> <u>ashamed</u> and <u>sorry</u> <u>for your participation</u> <u>in</u> <u>apostasy</u> <u>against</u> **𐤀𐤉𐤄𐤆**! Not only have you and your family lived the lies yourself, but you have led innocent sheep under your care deeper and deeper into apostasy against **𐤀𐤉𐤄𐤆** and **O𐤅𐤉𐤄𐤆**! If you can't teach the undiluted truth where you are, then leave that profession and get another job to make a living! But it's not over until it's over! Repent while there's still time to repent and walk in Yahuah's ways! If you continue to refuse to repent, then you and your family are really no different that the prophets of Baal! Like them you will face total destruction in the Lake of Fire, if you do not change! **It's still not too late!** After a couple of years with that Messianic group, I could no longer tolerate the observance of the unless traditions of men, while many weightier Commandments of **𐤀𐤉𐤄𐤆** were being ignored! No one, but me saw any harm in observing the pagan holidays along with Yahuah's festivals or the harm in suppressing Yahuah's name! I had to leave those sheep, but we had no place to go! So what should we do? Our family had decided once and for all to follow **𐤀𐤉𐤄𐤆** and **O𐤅𐤉𐤄𐤆**, even if no one else did! Of course we know that right now there are tens of thousands of overcomers all over the earth, who have similar stories! We are very thankful that **𐤀𐤉𐤄𐤆** has been so merciful to us! **𐤀𐤉𐤄𐤆** called us to follow Him and **we have answered His call**! However, we have found the Way of **O𐤅𐤉𐤄𐤆** to be very, very narrow and very <u>hard pressed</u>!

Tears in a Bottle

Yahushua's Way is hard pressed and full of tribulations, rejections, sorrows, and afflictions! Very few people <u>choose</u> to travel that Way!

Matthew 7

[13]*"Enter in through the narrow gate! Because the gate is wide – and the way is broad – that leads to destruction, and there are many who enter in through it.* [14]*"Because the gate is narrow and the way is hard pressed which leads to life, and there are few who find it.*

At this time we have our own family Shabbat times and our own Festival times! Vicki and I teach Yahuah's ways to our children everyday as we encounter the problems that arise <u>that</u> day! We have recently learned of a few other families in our area, who also serve ᴀYᴀZ with their whole heart! HalleluYah! HalleluYah! HalleluYah! I have been asking ᴀYᴀZ for some like minded friends!

During our spiritual journey, we made stops in the Baptist and the Full Gospel denominations of Christianity! Then we made a stop in Messianic Judaism, but we knew in our hearts that something was still missing! At each one of those stops, we met many kind individuals, who were doing what they truly believed was right at the time! At each stop we noticed that more and more people got off the narrow Way of OWYᴀZ! We have felt more and more alone as we have continued along on our journey! The good news is that as we have traveled the way of ᴀYᴀZ, we have fallen more and more in love with ᴀYᴀZ and OWYᴀZ! Now we want Yahuah's plans and desires to be completely fulfilled in our lives as well as in the lives of all Yahuah's overcomers, Israel! Doesn't ᴀYᴀZ, who fashioned our hearts and minds have the capability of experiencing feelings and desires? Doesn't ᴀYᴀZ feel joy, happiness, and gratification? Well, of course ᴀYᴀZ can, and to degrees that we cannot even imagine! My heart's desire is that my family would **exceed** Yahuah's own expectations and desires for us, if that's possible! We would like to totally fulfill Yahuah's desires for our family and gratify His heart beyond measure!

By the way, ᴀYᴀZ miraculously healed Christian of Perthes Disease, while we were in Dr. Bailey's office at the University Hospital in Augusta! Christian had been in traction for three months and was missing the 1st grade! I had prayed in my prayer room that even though I didn't understand why Christian had to have the disease, I understood that Christian belonged to ᴀYᴀZ! Christian's father submitted to Yahuah's will <u>that</u> night! Whatever was to be Yahuah's will, I knew that I could accept it because I knew in my heart that ᴀYᴀZ truly loved Christian **even more than I did!**

Tears in a Bottle

A few days later, I literally carried Christian as usual up to the ninth floor of the hospital for his scheduled appointment! The nurses took Christian back for X-rays as usual, but this time it took about 45 minutes for them to come back, when normally an X-ray took about 20 minutes! When they did come back, Dr. Bailey asked Christian, "Are you going to play baseball this summer?" Christian looked perplexed and said, "No sir, I can't!" Dr. Bailey asked Christian, "Why can't you play?" Christian looked confused and said, "Because of my hip!" Then Dr. Bailey said to Christian, **"What if I said that you can play baseball, if you promise me that you will hit a .400 batting average!"** Dr. Bailey told us that <u>miraculously</u> there was absolutely <u>no</u> sign of Perthes disease in Christian's hips and femur bones, which they verified by taking two sets of x-rays! Christian walked out of the hospital on his own two legs that day and has been playing baseball and hitting .400 ever since! Chad still has Juvenile Diabetes **<u>for the</u> <u>moment</u>** because ⊐Y⊐Z is still **using the pressure of that struggle to accomplish His purposes** in all of our lives! But I have asked ⊐Y⊐Z to let me see with my own two eyes, when He heals Chad from that disease! HalleluYah! HalleluYah! HalleluYah!

Well, that's the quick version of the Bragg's spiritual journey to this point! Even though I am <u>not</u> a polished writer, as you can certainly see, I was convicted that I must write *Let My People Go* for Yahuah's overcomers, **Israel**! I believe in the end the right people will read *Let My People Go* and Yahuah's purposes will be accomplished in their lives as well! HalleluYah! HalleluYah! HalleluYah! The Bragg family's message to all of Israel, is to **finish this race of patient endurance well! WE love you very, very much!**

The Two Ways

Matthew 7
[13]"Enter in through the narrow gate! Because the gate is wide – and the way is broad – that leads to destruction, and there are many who enter in through it. [14]"Because the gate is narrow and the way is hard pressed which leads to life, and there are few who find it.

Deuteronomy 30
[15]"See, I have set before you today life and good, and death and evil, [16]in that I am commanding you today to love 𐤉𐤄𐤅𐤄 your Elohim, to walk in His ways, and to guard His commands, and His laws, and His right-rulings. And you shall live and increase, and 𐤉𐤄𐤅𐤄 your Elohim shall bless you in the land which you go to possess. [17]"But if your heart turns away, and you do not obey, and shall be drawn away, and shall bow down to other mighty ones and serve them, [18]"I have declared to you today that you shall certainly perish, you shall not prolong your days in the land which you are passing over the Yarden to enter and possess. [19]"I have called the heavens and the earth as witnesses today against you: I have set before you life and death, the blessing and the curse. Therefore you shall choose life, so that you live, both you and your seed, [20]to love 𐤉𐤄𐤅𐤄 your Elohim, to obey His voice, and to cling to Him – for He is your life and the length of your days – to dwell in the land which 𐤉𐤄𐤅𐤄 swore to your fathers, to Abraham, to Yitshaq, and to Ya'aqob, to give them."

Dead Sea Scrolls (4Q473)
...and He has placed [before you] t[wo] ways, one which is goo[d and one which is evil. If you choose the good way], He will bless you. But if you walk in the [evil] way, [He will curse you]...

Acknowledgements

Restored Name King James Version

The Scriptures, Institute of Scripture Research

Book of Adam and Eve, Restored Name Version from R. H. Charles

American Leprosy Missions, http://www.leprosy.org/LEPdisease.html

My Jubilation Ministries, http://www.myjubilation.org/welcome.html

The Dead Sea Scrolls, Gerza Vermes

Who Wrote the Dead Sea Scrolls, Norman Golb

The Blue Letter Bible, http://www.blueletterbible.org/